D1557255

Concept Audits

Concept Audits

A Philosophical Method

Nicholas Rescher

LEXINGTON BOOKS
Lanham • Boulder • New York • London

Published by Lexington Books
An imprint of The Rowman & Littlefield Publishing Group, Inc.
4501 Forbes Boulevard, Suite 200, Lanham, Maryland 20706
www.rowman.com

Unit A, Whitacre Mews, 26-34 Stannary Street, London SE11 4AB

British Library Cataloguing in Publication Information Available

Library of Congress Cataloging-in-Publication Data
Names: Rescher, Nicholas, author.
Title: Concept audits : a philosophical method/Nicholas Rescher.
Description: Lanham : Lexington, 2016.
Identifiers: LCCN 2016023402 (print) | LCCN 2016024501 (ebook) |
    ISBN 9781498540391 (cloth : alk. paper) | ISBN 9781498540407 (Electronic)
Subjects: LCSH: Methodology. | Concepts.
Classification: LCC BD241 .R425 2016 (print) | LCC BD241 (ebook) |
    DDC 121/.4—dc23
LC record available at https://lccn.loc.gov/2016023402

Printed in the United States of America

For John Greco

Contents

Preface

I projected this book in the spring of 2015 and wrote most of it over that summer. Its aim is to answer the question of what remains of "ordinary language philosophy" and to show that this historic philosophical program still has to offer something of ongoing value in philosophy.

I am, as usual, indebted to Estelle Burris for invaluable help in putting my manuscript material into a form suitable for publication.

Nicholas Rescher
Pittsburgh, PA
January 2016

Part I

METHODOLOGY

Introduction

The Concept Auditing Process

CONCEPT AUDITING

This book expounds a certain distinctive methodology of philosophical investigation which could be characterized as *concept auditing*. Its aim is to determine if the treatment of a given philosophical issue has made appropriate use of the conceptual resources afforded by the pre-systemically established employment of the relevant concepts. For in the end, the philosopher has really no alternative but to respect the ground rules of ordinary usage—principally for two reasons: (1) because it is in relation to those meanings and usages that the problems of philosophy arises, and (2) because no matter what innovations and variables he would like to introduce it is in terms of those meanings and usages that he will have to give his initial explanations of what he is proposing to do. The task of a concept audit is accordingly to see to it that the conceptual resources put at a philosopher's disposal by that pre-established usage have been adequately employed and the prevailing distinctions and connections duly acknowledged. When a philosopher puts an everyday-life conception on the agenda—be it truth, knowledge, justice, beauty, or whatever, and purports to be dealing with what this involves he must know the correlative established rules of conceptual engagement. The relevant distinctions must be heeded, the pertinent relationships must be acknowledged, the operative implications must be maintained—all of the prevailing conventionalities must be honored. And the task of a concept audit is to ascertain that this is actually being done.

The mission of *financial* auditing is to verify that all *financial* business has been appropriately managed, with all use of *financial* resources correctly recorded and all transactions properly accounted for. Exactly the same situation is obtained when the "financial" of the preceding sentence is changed to "conceptual." For the mission of conceptual auditing is to verify that all conceptual business has been appropriately managed, with all use of resources properly substantiated and all transactions properly accounted for. For when philosophers address ideas that are embedded in established usage and purport to discuss *that sort of thing*, then they must be careful to honor the correlative understandings. The aim of concept conditioning is to check up on this. Though this is only one procedure among many in philosophical deliberation, it occupies a place of historical prominence and ongoing importance.

In cultivating this methodology one begins by examining the actual usage of a (philosophically relevant) term in the language of everyday-life discourse. But this essentially philological-lexicographic concern for the empirical realties is just the starting point. For one now turns in another direction to inquire into the (implicit) preconditions and presuppositions that are at work in enabling this mode of usage to realize with efficacy and efficiency the communicative functions for which it is instituted.

The methodology of philosophical concept audits accordingly involves three principal steps or phases:

1. Examining the proprieties of the employment of ordinary-language terms that figure significantly in a philosophical deliberation. One then moves from terms to concepts by—
2. Inferring on this basis the principles standardly at work in this usage—the presuppositions and presumptive consequence that constitute the rationale of the employment of this pre-systematic terminology. And one then goes on to—
3. Applying these findings to check that justice has been done to these principles in the philosophical deliberations at issue or if they have been violated in some way.

Overall, the process is designed to check that insofar as a philosophical thesis or doctrine makes use of some concept which—like knowledge or wisdom or duty—has a pre-philosophically established nature, those philosophical deliberations stay on topic. It is, after all, constructive to ensure that a philosophical discussion has expended wisely and sensibly the deposit of presumptions and presuppositions that shape its terminology.

It is a basic principle of rational communication that words are to be used in their standard signification and that sentences are being used to say what they mean. The philosopher too is, like anyone else, bound by this. Unless explanations to the contrary are provided, one is entitled to believe that in philosophical discussion concepts that have a well-established extra-philosophical usage continue to function subject to the correlative conditions, presumptions and implications that prevail elsewhere. The task of a perceptual audit is to ascertain that this basic principle is honored—and not violate—in a philosopher's discussions.

There can be little doubt about the utility of such a procedure. The concepts that figure centrally in philosophical deliberations are always borrowed from everyday life or from its elaboration in science. The discussions of philosophy always maintain some connection to these pre- or extraphilosophical notions; they cannot simply rid themselves of those standard conceptions that are the flesh and blood of our thinking in everyday life. The philosopher's "knowledge" and "ignorance," his "right" and his "wrong" must be those of ordinary people—or at least keep very close to them. His "space" and "time" and "matter" must be those of the natural scientist. In abandoning the concepts of our pre-philosophical concerns in favor of word creations of some sort, the philosopher thereby also abandons the problems that constitute the enterprise's very reason for being. To talk *wholly* in terms of technical concepts that differ from the ordinary ones as radically as the physicist's concept of *work* differs from the plain man's notion is in effect to change the subject. And whatever appeal this step may have, it is not one that we can take *within* the framework of the professed objective enlightenment about the issues. It is neither candid nor helpful to pass off the wolf of concept abandonment as the sheep of concept elucidation. The reader of a philosophical discussion rightly expects that when it purports to address the issues revolving around a familiar concept such as justice or knowledge or duty it does not change the subject. When he finds that it actually deals with something quite detached and different, he has every reason to feel defrauded.

The rationale of concept auditing in philosophy thus roots in the clearly sensible idea that before one can profitably investigate the tenability of a philosophical doctrine it is needful to ascertain the meaning and thereby the meaningfulness and coherence of the conceptions in whose terms those doctrines are formulated. It is, after all, hard to argue with the idea that in philosophy as elsewhere we need to become clear—ultimately even if not individually—about just what it is that we are talking about and what we intend to say about it. Granted, clarity is not enough but it is nevertheless indispensable.

Take as simple a term as the conjecture "and." It clearly admits of a variety of distinct and different uses, as per

- the *consequential* and, effectively for "and therefore": He was found guilty and fined a penalty.
- the *temporal* and, effectively for "and then": He took off his coat and went into the kitchen.
- the and of *combination*: He drank a scotch and soda.
- the and of *prolongation*: As he talked on and on our boredom went on and on.

"And" comparatively admits of different construal, since there are virtually as many senses of "and" as there are modes of supplementation. Anything but misunderstanding would result for mistaking one for another.

And this situation is not without philosophical relevance. For example, when the Greek atomists said that their atoms were indivisible and indestructible were they conjoining two distinct features or was their and here consequential? That is, did they intend to say that the atoms were indestructible because they are indivisible, in that dividing and dissolution into components is the only possible mode of destruction operative in nature. Thus, properly understanding the terminology of philosophical discourse—be it everyday or technical on orientation—is essential to judging the acceptability of theses and theories at issue.

POROUS GENERALIZATIONS

Concept audits are partially needed in philosophizing because an inherent tendency to conceptual anomaly is endemic in this domain's penchant for generalization. Philosophy thrives on generalization. A general statement of the form "A's are (are not) B's" admits of two alternative constructions. One is the *universalistic* reading: "Invariably and exceptionlessly, all/no A's are B's." The other is the *standardistic* reading: "Standardly and ordinarily, A's are (are not) B's." To say the latter is tantamount to saying that A's are (are not) B's *as a rule*, recognizing that this rule, like most, may admit of exceptions. On this sort of reading, statements of a general form are to be construed not with *strict* universality, but in a porous manner, where exceptions can step through the cracks, as it were, because the generality is one of how matters stand normally, standardly, and "in the usual course of things." And so taken, the acceptability of standardistic generalizations is not at odds with the recognition of exceptions of various kinds. The generality of standardistically construed generalizations is an imperfect one: they are not literally and strictly universal, but are subject to a qualification on the lines of standardly/customarily/as a rule as opposed to holding always/invariably/exceptionlessly. The problem is that philosophy—like law—seeks a precision and rigor that everyday life generally eschews in the interests of easier communication. And so there is bound to be a tension between the thought and reasoning of the philosopher and that of everyday life. It is difficult to manage the pursuit of precision by means of ideas and statements geared to the proceedings of porous generalization. And this produces an inevitable tension. Philosophy requires exact definition where ordinary practice settles for explanations of how matters stand "as a rule." Philosophy demands exact boundaries where ordinary language generally affords only indefinite and shadowy ones.

The discrepancies and frictions that arise between the conceptual machinery of everyday-life discourse and philosophical deliberations imposes a special burden on the philosopher where he addresses issues and problems that are formed in the terminology of everyday discourse. For then he must explain himself. In fitting everyday conceptions into the theoretical framework of his doctrines—removing them from one context of usage into an environment that is significantly different—he assumes the burden of explanation and clarification. And the object of conceptual auditing is to check that this obligation has been adequately discharged and that a philosopher's recourse to everyday terms and concepts has been brought into adequate explanatory alignment with the use that is actually made of them in philosophical discussion.

To illustrate this we shall briefly anticipate the discussion of section 4 below.

The idea of knowledge so functions in standard usage that one must be certain of what one claims to know. But ordinary discourse envisions certainty as something that can be realized effectively in a practicable way: It does not construe that certainty is so rigorist and demanding a manner as something so categorical and absolute as to transcend any and all prospect of its reasonable realization. An overly rigoristic conception would make knowledge unachievable and open the door to skepticism. But when a philosopher's hyperbolic conception of the matter fails to reckon with what actually passes for certainty in everyday usage, nothing but trouble can ensue.

Accordingly, another characteristic task of concept auditing is to monitor the standards of usage in regard to the proper range of application of a concept, for example by mentioning the due directive between literal and figurative, metaphysical, or analogical applications. It can often prove illuminating to treat one thing as another—say an organism as a mechanism. Thus, Descartes found it instructive to treat various philological process of organisms mechanical—by viewing the heart as a pump, for exemplifying. But the mechanization of organisms has to be kept within limits. And not sketched to the point to which some Cartesians carried it by denying feelings to crucial and maintaining that they could not possibly suffer pain.

The Rationale of Concept Auditing

As will be amply illustrated by the diversified concept audits to be surveyed below, matters can readily go awry with philosophical deliberations through failing to honor the ground rules that govern the meaning and interconnections of terms. In departing from the standing conventions and tacitly changing the subject, a philosophical position will compromise both its intelligibility and its cogency.

Science has the luxury of being able to define its terms operationally. It can say things on the order of

- When you proceed in such-and-such a way to carry out such-and-such measurements, the result is the *gravitational mass* of an object.
- When you carry out such-and-such calculations with the number of births in the population the result is the *birth rate*.

In science one can accordingly explain one's terminology not via further terminology, but via procedures. Philosophy does not have this option. It must explain its terminology in terms of pre-existing terminology and human intelligibility in the acting language of everyday discourse. Its need to serve understanding commit it to heeding terminological ground rules of our pre-systematic talk.

Granted, different enterprises and diverse realms have their own technical language each with its own usages. Be it in medicine, wine-connoisseurship, cricket, philosophy, or natural science different domains have different vocabularies and modes of discourse. Take wine lore. Here *dryness* is no opposite of *wetness* and has nothing to do with the fluidity of the wine but rather is a matter of lack of sweetness. And "full body" has nothing to do with shape and avoirdupois. Even when the same terms are used, the technical language of a domain can veer away from the conception of ordinary usage. And it would be absurd to ask "What is the real meaning of 'sweetness'—that of the wine connoisseur or that of the ordinary man-in-the-street?"

When a philosopher uses the terminology of everyday discourse does this employment accord with the proprieties of established usage? Does he use those terms in their accepted sense or has he effectively changed the subject without due explanation? Is he committing some sort of terminological misapprehensions?

There is nothing inherently wrong with changing the established ground rules of discourse through which concept is conveyed. But providing an explanation of and motivation for the purposed move is always incumbent on the mover. And that explanation and motivation must be provided in pre-systematically intelligible terms. It cannot itself deploy conceptual revisions whose credentials are as yet unestablished and in question. Accordingly, one prime object of conceptual auditing is to determine if some sort of conceptual chicanery or fraud is being committed in a philosophical discussion.

Category Mistakes

One of the most significant results of a concept audit is the detecting of *category mistakes,* which constitutes one of the most notorious modes of malfeasance of the management of concepts.

When, where, and how did the idea of carbon originate? Did it exist in the first nanosecond of the universe, where there were as yet no carbon atoms? Did it originate when humans discovered that there was such a thing as carbon? All of these questions make no viable sense. They are all fallacies in being predicated in the false and untenable presupposing that an idea such as that of carbon is somehow spatiotemporal. They are on the order of asking for the color of triangularity or the origination time of the number 3.

All such questions are predicated on erroneous presuppositions. Numbers (unlike plants) are not the sort of things that have color. Numbers (unlike butterflies) are not the sort of thing that have an origin. It makes no sense to temporalize ideas—or to ask when and how they originated. We cannot ask if the idea of gold antedated the conception of gold by humans.

The endeavor to emplace ideas in the space-time order of actual things is also pre-ordained to failure, seeing that their very identity places ideas outside the framework of space-time. It makes no sense to spatialize ideas—to contemplate a region or world of ideas. They simply are not the sorts of things that have locations in this or any other realm of things. To claim otherwise is to commit the mistake of applying to and not of thing conceptions that only hold elsewhere. Trees have size, but odors do not; odors have intensity, but trees do not. Animals have age and location but numbers do not. To think of ideas in spatiotemporal terms (asking about their age or location) is a category mistake on the order of inquiry what the color of numbers or the shape of forgetfulness.

In the sense now at issue *ideas* do not admit spatiotemporal characterization. They neither originate not prevail nor yet have "existence" in some domain of their own. Their mode of being does not fall into the usual range of consideration. Like mathematical operations such as subtraction or division you cannot assign to them a spatial location nor yet ask when they originated in time. They are not eternal or sempiternal—they are literally timeless. Time (and space) neither includes nor excludes them. By their very nature they lie beyond the temporal pale. To think of them in spatiotemporal terms is to make a category mistake on the order of inquiring into the shape or color of a legal right.

The detection of such inappropriate violations of the understandings and presumptions that constitute the established guidelines for a philosophically relevant idea is one of the most characteristic and significant outcomes of conceptual auditing.

Closing Observations

Numerous specific instances of practice generally precedes the identification of general modes of proceeding. People spoke grammatically before anyone conceived of grammar. People engaged in counting things before anyone conceived of arithmetic. Analogously, philosophical theorists have conducted concept audits before this was conceived of as a systemic process. Particular instances of the procedure go far back in the history of philosophy, even though the identification of a generic method may be a johnny-come-lately. And it is striking how widely this method has been applied. As the following pages will show, while the method of conceptual and thus procedurally uniform its range of application and implementation have manifested a great deal of thematic variation.

Consider an illustration. The conception of *lying* as we ordinarily deal with it is rather loose and equivocal. It hovers undecidedly over the reasoning:

1. To tell a falsehood
2. To tell a falsehood wittingly (i.e., realizing that it is false)
3. To tell a falsehood wittingly and with deceptive intent
4. To tell a falsehood wittingly and with malign deceptive intent

The theorist who has an ax to grind—who wishes, say, to argue that lying is always morally reprehensible—has a job of work to do. He cannot simply suppose that only construal (4) alone constitutes "real lying" and then rely on malign deceptive intent to do his work for him. He cannot ride roughshod over the ambiguities of that pre-established conception. And if he tried to do so a conceptual audit can and should bring to light the questionable nature of his proceedings through a doctrinally convenient gerrymandering of the term.

But at this point someone may well object:

"But all this obeisance of established usage is totally misplaced. Philosophy should not respect outdated ways of thinking. Its mission is one of enlightenment, of freeing us outmoded beliefs, obsolete convictions, inherent superstition, dated popular misconceptions, and the like."

All this may well be so: it is, at any rate, deserving of consideration. But in the present context it is beside the point. For our concern here is not with knowing historically established beliefs and doctrines, but with the present use of established terms. For here it is the meaning of terms and not the advocacy of doctrinal position that is at issue. The point is that if when philosopher purports to be addressing an issue that is focused in established meaning of words, however radically he may want to distance himself from doctrinal positions often or even generally maintained about the matter. If he proposes to revise our views about something (say the X's) he must still heed the circumstance that it is those things (the X's as we standardly conceive of them) that his deliberations propose to address. So in this regard he must continue to be "on the same page" as the rest of us.

Concept auditing, then, is a process that is applicable and useful throughout a wide range of philosophical contexts. But the best way to exhibit applicability is to proceed to apply it widely and effectively. And exactly this is the mission of the remainder of the book. In the course of providing a host of illustrations of concept audits it not only manifests the utility and fruitfulness of the method, but engages with a wide variety of philosophical deliberations that are of considerable interest and instruction in and of themselves.

Quis custodiet ipsos custodes: who watches the watchers themselves? There is nothing sacrosanct about audits as such: the business of auditing can itself be well- or ill-managed. The idea of second-level auditing—of checking up on how well the auditors have done their business—makes perfectly good sense. But this is something which, in their present case, will be left as an exercise for the reader, who will himself have to judge if there are any defects in the numerous concept audits that are now going to be presented in these pages.

Part II

SOME HISTORICAL APPLICATIONS

The Socratic Method as an Illustration

SOCRATIC METHOD

An instructive instance of concept auditing is provided in Book I of Plato's *Republic* with its focus on the nature of justice. Here one of the dialogue's characters, Polemarchus, endorses the widely accepted position that justice consists in giving every person their due (*suum ciuique tribuere*)—so that justice quintessentially requires returning someone what they have entrusted into your keeping.[1]

In opposition, Socrates argues that this cannot be seen as an adequate account, resting his case on the must-be pre-theoretical considerations regarding what is right and just. For it is clear that being treated justly must be beneficial, and this is out of line with this purported explanation. And this would be counterindicated by returning his weapons to someone who is evidently unhinged and frantically intent on self-destruction or returning his money to someone who is inebriated and "on a tear" at gambling.

The ruling idea here is that our pre-theoretical understanding of a philosophically germane concept has to be honored by any truly adequate account of its nature. Accordingly, any philosophical theses regarding a concept that has consequences at odds with its established understanding must for this very reason be rejected.

RAMIFICATIONS

There are, of course, linguistic issues that established usage cannot decide exactly because circumstances change. Is the captain of an airship entitled to the same privileges, responsibilities, and obligations as the captain of a sea-ship? He should certainly be responsible for ensuring the safety and security of the crew and the passengers, but beyond that lies an open range of issues which conceptual auditing can do but little to resolve. But when pre-theoretical considerations are clear, philosophical discourse must favor them. Established usage demands respect on matters of conceptualization and has to be duly honored accordingly.

The detection by conceptual audits of failures of the failure of proposed theories to honor the established standards for philosophically instructive concepts justice, truth, knowledge, beauty, and the like, is a characteristic feature of the "Socratic Method" at work in Plato's early dialogues. For here Socrates' mode of inquiry is in essence a dialectical procedure designed to show how some naive construal of a philosophically significant concept goes awry. The upshot is not the positive result of establishing how the philosophically relevant terminology at issue (justice, courage, piety, truth, knowledge, etc.) is properly to be used, but rather negative finding that they cannot sustain some claim to *explain* what the terms "really mean" by some sort of definition or formula.

Here Socrates' discussion partners acted as amateur philosophers in purporting some generalities about the matter of philosophically significant conceptions such as justice, knowledge, or nature. Throughout, Socrates proceeds by way of an *elenchus*, a "putting to the test" by way of a question/answer dialectic designed to determine whether the proposed account squares with the established employment of the terms at issue. By raising questions that manifest discrepancies from what we would naturally want to say, Socrates in effect concluded a concept audit able to show that for the most part those theoretical proposals just do not work. By ingenious interrogations he made it clear that they simply do not provide for what one would want and have to say about a philosophical matter on the basis of the pre-systematically established conception of its issues.

NOTE

1. Plato, *Republic*, 331D-336A.

Neo-Platonic Wholes

NEO-PLATONISM ON WHOLES

Among the many philosophical contributions of the Platonic Academy of classical antiquity was a significantly informative insight into the nature of wholes. For the ancient Platonists stressed that a true whole has logicoconceptual priority over its parts because it provides the defining principle of integration that unifies those constituents into being *its* parts.[1] As Plotinus put it in the *Enneads*: "That which is truly a whole (*to alêthôs pan*) has not been assembled from the parts, but has itself generated those parts, and is in this way alone truly a whole."[2] And on this basis, these thinkers stressed that there is a need to distinguish between authentic *Wholes* and mere *Assemblages*.

The distinction at issue is illustrated by the contrast that between an animal or plant whose parts have no independent existence, and a stone wall or even a flock of birds, whose independently existing parts are fortuitously brought together to combine—accidentally, as it were—to form what is at best a quasi-whole. Accordingly, a machine would qualify as a Whole because its parts exist only in order to play their role within its context, while a heap of sand would not be a genuine Whole because its parts have an entirely independent existence, and their coordination obtained by chance rather than principle. And a well-written story would be a Whole because its parts are coordinated by a desirable plot line, whereas a sequence of disjointed sentences will not be a Whole owing to the absence of a unifying principle to determine its parts as such. The contrast between a formal garden and uncultivated landscape also illustrates the same distinction. Or again the set of odd numbers 1, 3, 5, 7, 9 would be an authentic Whole because its membership is unified on the basis of an obvious generative rationale, while the set of random numbers 15, 376, 897, 2, 5, 6, would not be a genuine Whole because no determinative principle is discernible.

In effect, neo-Platonic theory took a concept audit of the part/whole idea to show that our understanding of the matter involved embodies an implicit distinction between what is genuinely and authentically a Whole, and what is so only seemingly—figuratively or analogically. Genuine wholes are not mere assemblages but embody a unifying a rationale or principle that functions at

THE VARIETY OF MODES OF INTEGRATION

X	Y	Z
pages	book	being bound together
species	genera	sharing a significant common feature
hours	day	chorological inclusion
provinces	country	legal arrangements
people	family	biological kinship
bricks	wall	physical integration
shards	vase	commonality of origin
episodes	story	authorship history
battles	war	historical continuity
cities	country	inclusion in national borders

Figure 3.1

the level of ideational rather than purely substantive considerations, along the lines exemplified in Figure 3.1.

MEREOLOGY AND ONTIC INTEGRITY

One way to elucidate the idea of an integrity of unification into a single whole is to proceed by posing the question:

> What is the feature Z that makes different Xs be parts (constituents, components) of one and the same Y?

Reflection on this question issue readily reveals that it will not admit of any single uniform answer. As the data of Figure 3.1 show, there is simply no commonality or uniformity to the unifying principle that integrates the parts into one single whole. For while in each case there indeed is some principle of unification at work to link the different subitems together into one single superitem, by means of a coordinative rationale, just what this is will vary markedly in the different cases. Thus what holds those Z's together is not *substantive* sameness but the functional commonality of *purposive sameness*, a factor that lies not in the physical but in the ideational realm. It was this considerations that made the analysis of wholes fit hand and glove into neo-Platonic doctrine.

METHODOLOGY

In deliberating along these lines, the neo-Platonists in effect employed the following sort of methodological procedure:

1. To begin by examining the actual usage of certain family of key terms. (In the present case: part/whole assemblage/constituent.)
2. To look within this range of usage for general principles and distinctions able to account for the prevailing relationships that underlie this way of proceeding.
3. To exploit this analysis to bring to light a philosophically significant feature implicit in the actualities of usage of those terms. (In terms of present case that a whole is not just a fortuitous assemblage of constituents but limits those parts together through conformity to a unifying principle.)

Such a concept auditing procedure serves to elucidate the idea underlying established usage in a way capable of yielding a philosophically instructive insight. And while a concept audit often has the negatively critical result of indicating philosophical violations of established usage, in the present case its result is positive, in bringing to light a philosophically instructive feature implicit in the proprieties of that established usage.

Applications

The neo-Platonists envisioned two important implementations and applications of their interpretation of strict wholeness.

The first is the application to the universe in its entirety. This, they maintained, is and ought to be seen as an authentic Whole and accordingly ought to have a rational plan or design that meaningfully integrates its consistent parts.

And a second significant application of the idea unfolded with regard to the life of a person. This too, so they held, should by rights be a properly integrated unit whose consistent component ought to fit together into a rational overall plan that endows the life of an individual with a coherent rational structure—an organic unification as it were. Just as the human body is a rationally integrated system, so should a human life be such that its description can constitute a coherently unfolding story whose parts are integrated through foreshadowings and consequences into meaningfully coherent whole. In this light integrity is a key venture and being "a person of integrity" is something to which every rational individual would do well to aspire.

NOTES

1. See Damian Caluori, *Plotinus on the Soul* (Cambridge: Cambridge University Press, 2015), p. 76.

2. Plotinus, *Enneads*, III, 7, 4, 9–11.

#4

Descartes and Generalization

CARTESIAN DOUBT

René Descartes (1592–1650) presented the following line of reasoning to support skepticism regarding human knowledge.

> [I] had accepted, even from my youth, many false opinions for true . . . and from that time I was convinced of the necessity of undertaking once in my life to rid myself of all the opinions I had adopted. . . . But to this end, it will not be necessary for me to show that the whole of these are false—a point, perhaps, which I shall never reach; . . . it will be sufficient to justify the rejection of the whole if I can find in each some ground for doubt. Nor for this purpose will it be necessary even to deal with each belief individually, which would be truly an endless labor; but, as the removal from below of the foundation necessarily involves the downfall of the whole edifice, I will at once approach the criticism of the principles on which all my former beliefs rested. All that I have, up to this moment, accepted as possessed of the highest truth and certainty, I received either from or through the senses. I observed, however, that these sometimes mislead us; and it is the part of prudence not to place absolute confidence in that by which we have even once been deceived.[1]

Descartes' warrant for this position was founded, not upon specific investigation of the individual merits or demerits of particular knowledge claims, but upon the wholesale calling into question of entire groups of claims on the basis of generic considerations, such as those regarding their subject matter or their source.

To begin with, however, it is necessary to recognize such "Cartesian doubt" for what it is, namely as an instance of a generic warrant for doubting. For it involves a procedure by which the claim of the doubtfulness of some

21

particular proposition p is supported by a highly generalized argument of the paradigm:

- Statements grounded on considerations of type T are sometimes false.
- p is grounded on the considerations C, which are of type T.

∴ p is dubious (i.e., might well be false).[2]

Accordingly, so Descartes here argued that our claims to knowledge are insecure overall because when uncertainly afflicts *each one* of our beliefs, it might, quite possibly, afflict *all* of them.

It is this particular reasoning that will concern us here. (The broader issue of skepticism-at-large reaches far beyond our present purview.)

MUSICAL CHAIRS

The present audit of Descartes' skepticism reasoning will focus solely in its use of the argument that what holds true for *each* could possibly hold true for *every*. And the realty of it is that this sort of reasoning is of very questionable soundness.

Consider the game of musical chairs. When the music stops any and every player can possibly be seated. But they cannot *all* possibly be seated—there just aren't enough seats. In a contended election any one of the candidates can be chosen. But not *all* of them.

Again consider entries in the decimal expansion of pi, say in particular the ten thousandth entry. Given our available information it is perfectly possible that this decimal place may turn out to be a zero. But it is certainly not possible that *all* of them should be zero, thereby having pi take exactly the value 3.

Put in standard logical notation, in such cases we have ("x)àFx but not à("x)Fx. The issue accordingly turns on the exact placement of that universal quantifier. What is possible for any one of the group need not—and generally will not be—possible for all of them together.

And—to return to Descartes—this holds with possible mistakes as well. In various matters of cognition we could possibly be wrong in *any one* particular case, but it is somewhere between implausible and impossible that we should be wrong in *all* of them. Smith's memory is shaky: the name of a particular person often eludes him. But that he should systematically have the whole lot vanish from his mind is simply too far-fetched.

And the same holds the other way round. There are simply too many entries in the dictionary for me to memorize all of them. Given the size of the *Oxford English Dictionary*, it is inevitable that there will be entries I will never memorize. But there is no single one that is unmemorizable for me—entries that I cannot possibly memorize. Even as we cannot automatically move from every to all, so we cannot move conversely form not-all to not-any. It is musical chairs over again.

THE BIG PICTURE

And so a careful concept audit with respect to the usage of any/all/every in relation to possibilities reveals that that particular Cartesian argument goes awry. The ground rules governing the employment of these concepts precludes his interpretation of the situation. Single-case possibilities just do not allow of universalized. Descartes' generalization argument does not work.

Moreover, a larger lesson looms in the background. Our knowledge is not built up like a children's block-tower where the removal of one constituent causes the whole structure to collapse. It is more like a stone wall, where the removal of one component can leave the overall structure substantially intact.

NOTES

1. René Descartes, *Discourse on Method*, tr. by John Veitch (London: Everyman's Library, 1912); my italics.
2. This generic argumentation for doubtfulness goes back to the ancient skeptics' assault on the stoic conception of decisive impressions (*katalêptikê phantasia*), arguing that it would suffice to show that a single decisive-seeming impression proves erroneous to establish that this whole domain is unreliable.

#5

Spinoza on Things and Ideas

SPINOZA'S THESIS

Those who are not outright Platonists by holding that ideas themselves exist as such in another realm of being, instead regard ideas as mental contrivances devised for their own purposes by thinkers. As Spinoza put it, "By *idea* I understand a conception of the mind which the mind forms because it is a thinking agent" (*Ethics* II, Definition 3). This fact makes it important to distinguish between ideas and things, because things are not in general creatures of the mind, even though they will doubtless be potential objects of mental conceptions. All this Spinoza very sensibly accepted.

But at this point, Spinoza made a very problematic move. For while he accepted that ideas are distinct from the things they represent, he nevertheless endorsed the doctrine that the *relationships* among ideas always mirror corresponding *relationships* among the objects. And in consequence he maintains that "The order and connection of ideas is the same as the order and connection of things" (*Ethics*, Book II, Paragraph 7). But this looks to be highly implausible.

THE PROBLEM

For example, let it be that cat is asleep on the mat. No problem there! But we can hardly say that the cat idea is snoozing on the mat idea. Ideas just do not relate to one another in the way in which things do. Things are interrelated in the order of space, time, and causality. But ideas are outside the world's physical order. The collision of billiard balls causes clicks. But there is no way in which ideas can produce noises.

24

Persons have birthplaces. But George Washington just did not become a Virginian through the connection of ideas, but by the doings of people. And not only do things and ideas not stand connected by the same relationships, but the structure of the relations at issue are quite different. (People are related genetically, places geographically, but ideas conceptually.)

Granted, in the realm of high abstraction—in pure mathematics, say—the things at issue are world-detached ideas and the relation among them are ideal in their nature. But in the real world of physical concreta a different situation prevails, since here the relations among things are substantive rather than ideal. With abstractions (say lines on a plane) it will doubtless be the case that the specifying ideas of them will determine how they are ordered and connected. But with concreta this will simply not be the case. When there are three billiard balls on the table, their arrangement yet remains an open issue.

As the matter is normally understood, thing-relationships (e.g., in space and time) and idea-relationships (e.g., by way of agreement or of conflict) involve different issues. Spinoza's doctrine of an identity of object-relations and idea-relations just cannot sustain a conceptual audit of the correlative terminology.

#6

Kantian Absolutism in Moral Theory

PRELIMINARIES

A good illustration of the philosophical importance of careful heed to the properties of the established usage of terms arises in the contrast between falsehood telling and lying.

In his classic little 1797 essay "On a Supposed Right to Lie from Philanthropy" Immanuel Kant argued that lying is always wrong,[1] maintaining that "to be honest in all declarations is a sacred command of reason prescribing unconditionally, one not to be curtailed by any conveniences" (8:427). To substantiate position he discussed the following sort of situation:

> You are visiting at the home of a friend who has a bitter enemy bent on his destruction. While he is downstairs in the wine cellar, his sworn enemy bursts in, drawn sword in hand, and shouts "Where is he?" Would you be entitled to say: "I have no idea; he just went out."

Conceding that from a casuistical point of view making this response might have a plausible *excuse*, Kant nevertheless maintained that it does not qualify as the exercise of a *right*. He emphatically insisted that you have no such right.

Designated as *rigorism*, Kant's insistence on moral correctness is almost universally decried by ethical theorists. But careful attention to terminology indicates that such a criticism of Kant's teaching is very problematic. For there is a terminologically grounded point of view—one closely linked to Kant's own doctrine—from which his idea that there is no such thing as a right to lie can be cogently and convincingly supported. The following deliberations will try to clarify how this is so.

ANALYSIS

Many human actions can proceed in an entirely value-neutral way that thereupon admits of a supplemental, morally laden qualification. Take killing someone. The soldier on the battlefield, the executioner on the gibbet, the automobile driver whose car has spun out of control on an oil slick, the pharmacist who inadvertently attached the wrong label to a drug, may all end up killing someone. But none of them is a murderer since murder is not just killing someone but rather killing someone with intentional malice. And in a similar way many otherwise morally neutral modes of action have normally inappropriate counterparts, as per the following series:

misleading someone/deceiving someone
bettering in a transaction/cheating in a transaction
disappointing someone/betraying someone
hitting someone/beating someone
injuring someone/harming someone
damaging something/vandalizing something

In each case the former can, in theory at least, occur without any moral culpability, whereas the latter involves a malignity of intent that automatically marks the so-described mode of action as something wicked and morally reprehensible. In each case, the first of the actions can and may well be ethically neutral, whereas the second mode of characterization always carries a prejudgment of moral impropriety built into its very mode of formulation. In taking an implicitly evaluative rather than the merely descriptive stance that second characterization effectively claims that the action at issue is morally reprehensible.

And in the matter now under consideration the critical point is that the person who tells a falsehood is not necessarily *lying* in anything like the literal sense of this term. For consider the contrast between telling a falsehood and lying is such that the former can be done inadvertently and even with the best of intentions. But lying by the very nature of the conceptualization at issue is telling a falsehood with morally malign intent. What one might be inclined to call "lying with benign intent" is really a contradiction in terms because that benign intent counterindicates the characterization of "lying." When careful usage is of the essence one would have to speak more guardedly of "misleading with benign intent" or even "sparing him the truth." And by its very formulation, the injunction "Never lie without having an adequate excuse" is a solecism—a contradiction in terms. For lying is (by definition) falsehood telling with maliciously deceptive intent. And if there were indeed an adequate excuse on this score then the intent is not in fact inappropriately deceptive.

CONCLUSION

And so while injunctions like, "Do not tell falsehoods," or "Do not kill" are discussible from a moral point of view, nevertheless, "Do not lie," or "Do not murder" are not. For in using the former mode of characterization in describing the situation the moral issue is settled and resolved.

As these deliberations indicate, the interests of philosophical cogency requires a significant contrast to be taken into account. It revolves around the distinction between

- Its *being excusable* for a person to act in a certain (inherently inappropriate) way

   and

- A person's *having a right* to act in this way.

When *X* uses his power over me to compel me (say by credibly threatening harm to my family or friends) to do something inherently wrong, I have an excuse for this transgression, but I certainly do not have a corresponding *right* for acting so. The terminological considerations at work in the Kantian controversy pivots on the crucial contrast between having reproach-mitigating excuses and exercising a right to what one is entitled. And in the light of this gain in terminological care and accuracy, the philosophical attack on "Kantian absolutism" becomes a very dubious proposition. There is really nothing wrong with Kant's insistence that people never have a *right* to lie.

On closer inspection, then, that oft-reproved Kantian absolutism seems to qualify as altogether plausible. It is, after all, owing always, everywhere, and for anyone to deceive someone with the interest to cause undeserved and needless harm to people.

It is one thing to have a viable *excuse* for some sort of wrongdoing, but something very different to have a right to engage in such practice. An excuse exists when what is being done, though perhaps wrong, is in the circumstance the least of the evils. But of course you will never have a right to do evil. When, as with Kant, due account is taken of motion the door to absolutism opens wide.

And so the upshot of a concept audit of the relevant terms issues in Kant's favor. Once careful attention is given to the proprieties of usage, it must be conceded that Kant was right in two points:

1. That there is never such a thing as an actual *right* to act in a morally inappropriate way. (At most and at best there may be a sufficient *excuse* for so doing.)

2. That in consequence there is no such thing as a right to lie (or murder or deceive, etc.)

One final admonition. In the passage quoted at the outset, Kant characterizes it as a sacred command of reason to be *wahrhaft* and *ehrlich*, that is *sincere* and *honest*. Now in fact *wahrhaft* also allows of being construed as *truthful* as well as *sincere/veracious/conscientious*. And this latter reading could be taken to mean that Kant intends to condemn telling a falsehood unqualifiedly. But this interpretation would be highly problematic, as is indicated not only by Kant's immediate explanation of the term *wahrhaft* as meaning *sincere*, but also by his commitment elsewhere to an elaborate program of casuistry that can concede conscientiousness even in the face of failures to tell the truth.[2]

NOTES

1. Immanuel Kant, *Practical Philosophy,* tr. Mary T. McGregor (Cambridge: Cambridge University Press, 1996), pp. 605–616.
2. Critics of Kant's moral philosophy would do well to pay clearer heed to his discussion of casuistry in his *Metaphysical Principles of Nature* (*Metaphysische Anfangsgründe der Tugendlehre*).

#7

Mill on Desirability

A KEY DISTINCTION

In his classic treatise on *Utilitarianism* the English philosopher and social critic John Stuart Mill (1806–1873) wrote:

> The only proof capable of being given that an object is visible, is that people actually see it. The only proof that a sound is audible, is that people hear it: and so of the other sources of our experience. In like manner, I apprehend, the sole evidence it is possible to produce that anything is desirable, is that people so actually desire it . . . . No reason can be given why the general happiness is desirable, except that each person, so far as he believes it to be attainable, desires his own happiness.[1]

But Mill's reasoning here is specious. An object is "visible" if it *can* be seen; a sound is audible if it *can* be heard. But in calling something *desirable* we do not intend to say that it *can* be desired but rather that it *should* be desired, that it *deserves* to be desired. And this by no means follows from the fact that people do desire it. After all, popularity does not evidentiate validity. People widely and perhaps even generally desire that their enemies should come to grief, but this does not mean that such vengefulness is appropriate.

The reality of it is that careful usage requires us to heed a significant distinction between two very different modes of desirability, namely:

- desirable in the descriptive sense of being *capable* of being desired and thereby manifested as such through the simple fact that someone desires it.
- desirable in the evaluative sense of being *worthy* of being desired—and thereby in a condition where the facts about people's actual desires becomes irrelevant.

30

In Mill's discussion, however, the premises have it that happiness is desirable in Sense 1, whereas the conclusion stakes a claim for happiness in Sense 2. The reasoning is clearly fallacious. Concept auditing shows that Mill is betting on the wrong horse.

AXIOLOGICAL IMPLICATIONS

Mill's error has larger ramifications. One of the principal issues in value theory (axiology) is that raised by the question:

> Is all value instrumental? Do all of the things that we deem valuable actually qualify as such only insofar as they facilitate the achievement of desired ends?

As is so often the case with philosophical questions, the answer has to be an indecisive *yes and no*. And this indecisiveness obtained—thanks to the neglect of a necessary distinction with respect to a pivotal conception—in this case is that of "desired ends."

Here once again we have to heed the distinction between *factual desires* relating to

—ends that *are in fact desired* by people

And *mature desirability* relating to

—ends that *deserve to be desired* in virtue of a positivity inherent in their nature

It is—or should be—clear that only in the second case does desire betoken value. For value is coordinated not with what we do (factually) desire but with what we should (normatively) desire—that is, with that which is desirable (in the sense of being worthy of being desired).

The reality of it is that desire does not create values. All sorts of value-less or indeed unworthy things may in fact be desired by people. Only when something is worthy of it will desire come into a connection with value.

In its original form the idea of value instrumentality was construed *reductively*, with value seen as the result of something non-normative and as merely *de facto* desired: things thus being seen to acquire them through being dismissed. But in fact the orientation of dependency is reversed: the relation is not reductive but productive, with things qualifying for desire through having value. That initially problematic question about value instrumentality is thus more or less automatically resolved. All genuine value is indeed instrumental because its appropriate realization would invariably foster the achievement of inherently desirable objectives.

And in this case serves to provide careful heed of the proprieties of pre-systematic discourse provides constructive insight into how a philosophically important concept should actually work.

NOTE

1. John Stuart Mill, *Utilitarianism*, Chap 4 (near the start).

Ordinary-Language Philosophy on the Nature of Knowing

AUSTIN'S PROGRAM

A good example of concept auditing emerges in the work of the Oxford philosopher John L. Austin (1911–1960), who was a leading member of the school of "Ordinary Language Philosophy." In his investigations Austin sought to extract philosophical lessons from examining how language is actually used in competently managed everyday communication. The guiding idea was that in philosophical deliberations "we must pay attention to the facts of *actual* language, what we can and cannot say, and *precisely* why."[1]

Austin believed that philosophers have fixated upon the role of language in transmitting information to the neglect of the great variety of other things that we do with language, overemphasizing its informative role to the neglect of other important language uses.

One thing, however, that it will be most dangerous to do, and that we are very prone to do, is to take it that we *somehow* know that the primary or primitive use of sentences must be, because it ought to be, statemental or constative, in the philosophers' preferred sense of simply uttering something whose sole pretension is to be true or false, and which is not liable to criticism in any other dimension. We certainly do not know that this is so.[2]

Austin complained that this tendency has misled some philosophers into an inappropriate transition from acts of saying, to "acts of knowing." But these, he maintained, are merely a linguistic (rather than optical) illusion because— so Austin argued—there simply are no such things.

Thus consider that activities in which persons can engage are represented by possible answers to the question: "What are you doing?" Here Austin stressed that there is an important contrast between verbs that can answer this question and verbs that cannot. Thus one can say: *I am engaged in—*

- running the race
- memorizing a name
- studying the calculus
- looking for my lost purse
- making a bet

But one cannot appropriately say: *I am engaged in—*

- winning the race
- remembering a name
- understanding the calculus
- finding my lost purse
- losing a bet

The former are *activities* that may well result in realizing the latter *states*, if pursued a successful conclusion. But those states represent are outcomes and not activities: they are not actions I am doing but the (possible) results or products thereof.

And Austin observed that just exactly this distinction between activity verbs and achievements verbs is operative in the present case because knowing is not an activity but an end-state, a possible outcome of activities like inquiring or studying. In proper usage you cannot say "I am knowing that 2 + 2 = 4." You can be engaged in *learning* something, but not in *knowing* it. The verb "to know" does not admit of a *present continuous tense* in correct English usage. And so to think and talk as though that there is such a thing as an "act, action, or activity of knowing" is to fall victim to a grammatical deception. In sum, knowledge is not a kind of activity but a possible end-state in which various sorts of activities like investigating or learning or memorizing can result.

Here, so Austin insisted, philosophers have fallen victim to linguistic illusions and theorists who deliberated about "acts of knowing" were caught up in a delusion. And on the basis of their examination of linguistic usage Austin and his congeners maintained philosophical confusion and error can often (and some extremists among his followers thought *always*!) be averted by proper heed of the linguistic niceties. In effect they maintained that careful conceptual audits can evert all sorts of philosophical errors.[3]

ACTS VERSUS STATES

In contrast to Austin's dismissal of "acts of knowing" it is of interest to note that some medieval schoolmen (Thomas Aquinas, for one) had contemplated what they called the "act of being" (*actus existendi*)—envisioning an action whose completion is actual existence. This clearly would be a rather unusual activity, because its result would be automatically achieved whenever it is engaged in (as would also be the case with the act of acting). For here the action and its end-state are automatically coordinated. Although such an idea might seem somewhat strange, it nevertheless would appear to be viable. For it makes sense (though perhaps only marginally) to answer a question of the format "What is X doing?" with the response "X is existing," or "X is engaged in being." Despite seeming strange such a response would seem to be not just meaningful but true. To be sure, it would open the way to the further question: "So X is engaged in being: but in being what?" This leads the topic from existence to essence, and would seem perfectly natural to the scholastics.[4]

But be that as it may, the fact remains that the suppositions that here are "acts of knowing" which cry out for psychological or phenomenological investigation is an invitation to wander off in a very problematic track.

NOTES

1. J. L Austin, *Philosophical Papers*, p. 37.

2. J. L. Austin, *How to Do Things with Words* (Harvard MA: Harvard University Press, 1962), p. 72.

3. Further relevant discussions includes: J. O, Urmson et al., "J. L. Austin" In R. Rorty (ed.), *The Linguistic Turn* (Chicago: University of Chicago Press, 1967); G. J. Warnock, *J. L. Austin* (London; New York: Routledge, 1989).

4. On these issues see Jean-Christophe Bardout, *Penser l'existence* (Paris: J. Vrin, 2013).

#9

Russell-Gettier on the Analysis of Knowledge

THE CLASSICAL FORMULA

Philosophers have long entertained the prospect of characterizing knowledge as *justified true belief*. This view harks back to Plato's dialogue *Theaetetus*, which maintains that true belief does not suffice for knowledge and goes on to propose that knowledge is a matter of true belief *based on a suitable rationale (logos) of justification.*[1] On this basis one would be led to the following formula:

(*K*)Knowing consists in having justified correct (or true) belief

The plausibility of this contention lies in two considerations. First, knowledge must indeed be true: when someone has a false belief one cannot say that he knows this claim, but would have to say that he only *thinks* that he knows it. And secondly, random guesswork is not knowledge even when it chances to be correct. Belief without any justification and coming "out of the blue" as it were, without any cogent ground or basis, it could hardly qualify as a knowledge of fact.

A CRITIQUE VIA COUNTEREXAMPLES

Plausible though it may look, formula (*K*) has in recent times been extensively criticized. On the basis of what is, in effect, a conceptual audit of its pivotal idea—beginning with Bertrand Russell's discussion in his 1912 *The Problems of Philosophy.*[2] Here Russell presented the following counterexample: (in a slightly different format) Smith rightly believes that the third US President was a Virginian (which Thomas Jefferson actually was) because Smith wrongly thinks that it was James Monroe (who indeed was a Virginian). Smith's belief is correct, and he has supporting grounds for holding it, but we could certainly not credit him with knowledge. It is, after all, only by luck, as it were, that he holds a correct belief in the matter. While his belief is in fact true, there is a fatal disconnection between what is actually the truth-ground of the belief and Smith's rationale for its acceptance. And so while both correctness/truth and justification/grounding may serve as necessary conditions for knowing they nevertheless appear to be insufficient. And this would mean that (*K*) as it stands really cannot qualify as an adequate analysis or definition of knowledge. So argued Bertrand Russell.

Russell's critique was revived in a 1963 paper by Edmund Gettier,[3] which evoked so large and diversified a response that the controversy over (*K*) has becomes as "the Gettier Problem."[4] Nevertheless this widely touted inadequacy of thesis (*K*) has its problems.

The principal counterexamples to (*K*) that have been canvassed in the literature can be sorted into two principal families of cases.

Type I Counterexamples

Let it be that the following four suppositions hold with respect to some contention *p*:

1. *X* believes *p*
2. *p* is true
3. *X* has justification for believing *p* in that it follows logically from something—say *q*—that he also believes, although in fact
4. *q* is false

Here *X* clearly has justification for believing *p*, since by hypothesis thus follows logically from something that he believes. And *p* is true, so that it is in fact a true, justified belief. Nevertheless, we would certainly not want to say that *X knows* that *p*, seeing that his (only) grounds for believing it are incorrect.

To illustrate this situation let it be that *X* believes that Jones is in the United States since he is in New York City (where he landed at Kennedy airport yesterday). In the meantime, however Jones has flown on to Los Angeles. *X* is thus right that Jones is in the United States, and he had grounds for this conviction (since he arrived there yesterday). But in the circumstances these grounds do not validate his conviction, and we would certainly not credit X with knowing that Jones is in the United States (which he indeed is, though for all X actually knows Jones could be in Mexico City by now). Thus while X has a true belief and has grounds for holding it, we would not and in the circumstances could not credit him with actual knowledge of the relevant facts. Those grounds of X's are probatively inadequate: they *suggest* his conclusion but do not *constrain* it.

Type II Counterexamples

Let it be that:

1. X believes p-or-q
2. q is true (and consequently p-or-q is also true)
3. X disbelieves q
4. X believes p-or-q, but does so (only) because he believes p
5. p is false

Here p-or-q is true. And X has justification for believing p-or-q since it follows from p which he believes. And since p-or-q is true—albeit in virtue of q's being true (when X actually disbelieves)—it follow that p-or-q is a true, justified belief of X's. Nevertheless, in the circumstances we would certainly not say that X knows that p-or-q, seeing that his sole grounds for believing it is once more something that is false. The difficulty here is that X holds the belief p-or-q which is justified for X because it follows from X's (false) belief that p, but is true just because q is true (which X altogether rejects).

To illustrate this situation let it be that:

1. X believes that Jefferson succeeded as president America's first president, George Washington.
2. X accordingly believes that Jefferson or Adams was the second American president, although he thinks that Adams was the third president.
3. Since Adams was in fact the second American president, X's belief that Jefferson or Adams was the second American president is indeed true

So X's (2) belief is indeed both true and justified. Nevertheless we would certainly not say that X *knows* this since his ground for holding this belief is simply false.

And so, counterexamples of these two sorts have been widely interpreted as constituting a decisive detail to the construal of knowledge along the lines of thesis (K).

But the reality of it is not quite so straightforward.

LESSONS: A CRUCIAL EQUIVOCATION

An important lesson to emerge from the preceding counterexamples is that knowledge cannot simply be a matter of having a true belief that is *somehow* justified, but rather would require having a true belief that is *appropriately* justified. It will not do for the knower to have some sort of evidential justification of what is accepted but that this justification must be probatively sufficient. For the problem with those counterexamples is that the grounds that lead their protagonist to adopt the belief just do not suffice to assure that that which is believed is actually the case.

But at this point careful consideration of the linguistic situation can do yeoman work. For the fact is that (*K*) as it stands is actually equivocal and can admit of two distinct interpretations:

(K_1) A belief qualifies as knowledge *when it is true and justified.* (Here the matter is one of having *some* justification—and this ball lies in the believer's court.)

(K_2) A belief qualifies as knowledge *when it is both true and ADEQUATELY justified,* that is *when its acceptance as true is appropriately justified.* (Here the matter is one of actually adequate justification—and this ball lies in the third party claimant's court.)

The crucial point with (K_2) is that when knowledge is here so characterized that for justification that belief must be accepted not only by its believer

• on grounds that *he* deems adequate

but additionally

• these grounds of his must be so cogent that *we* (the attributers of the belief) also endorse them adequate.

For subjective justification (of the former sort) is one thing and objective justification (of the latter sort) is another and just this second is critical for knowledge.

The Siamese bonze who had never experienced winter, and for whom freezing conditions are wholly outside the range of available experience, had ample justification for believing that winter never assumes a condition of hardness where heavy men can simply walk on it. Nevertheless his belief was not objectively justified—in particular because we ourselves are justified in rejecting it. Objective justification must hold not just for the believer, but for any other duly informed individual.

And now when (K) is construed as per (K_2) counterexamples of the sort invoked by Russell and Gettier will not successfully tell against it because all of them lack critical factors for adequate justification. The basic idea of the (K) thesis is thus perfectly sound. It is just a matter of giving it an appropriate construal as invoking justification that is not just subjective but also objectively cogent as well. And so as far as the extensive literature on the subject is concerned, there is nothing fatal to the knowledge characterization of (K) provided that it is construed in the conditional manner of (K_2) rather than in the conjunctive manner of (K_1). A properly managed conceptual audit saves the day for (K).

A VARIANT PERSPECTIVE

A variant perspective on the matter is also instructive.

Like claims about anything else, claims about knowledge can be mistaken. I may be mistaken in claiming "Smith knows that p" though having based by contention on insufficient evidence. For example, the evidence at my disposal may simply be that p is true, and that X believes it to be so. A good deal is still missing here. For as we have seen, what is missing is just exactly that Smith holds this belief on grounds that are adequate and sufficient.

But now let us suppose a situation where this condition is absent and all that we have is:

(1) Smith accepts p
(2) Smith has grounds for accepting p
(3) p is true

In these circumstances, cognitive generosity may induce us to concede that people generally have adequate and sufficient grounding for their beliefs. And addition of this enthymematic premise would suffice to carry us over from those given premises to the fullness of actual knowledge. In effect we can see the step from (1)–(3) to actually knowing as an enthymematic inference that is valid in the presence of a plausible but missing enthymematic premiss.

So if we are looking for a *plausible evidential basis* for ascribing knowledge (in a community of rationale inquirers), then justified true belief as per (K) will do the job. But if we are looking for a *coordinately equivalent characterization* of knowing—a possible definition of the concept—then, only K_2 provides for the requisite necessary and sufficient (rather than merely evidential) conditions.

The point is that there is an inductive gap between (K)-style "knowledge" and the more sophisticated construal of K_2. Here once again careful heed of properties of established usage can serve to resolve a phenomenologically controverted issues in a plausible and cogent manner. A concept audit of the relevant terminology can successfully defend the classical Platonic conception of knowledge against its latter-day critics.

NOTES

1. Plato, *Theaetetus* 201C-210D.
2. Bertrand Russell, *The Problems of Philosophy* (London and New York: Oxford University Press, 1912), pp. 205–206.
3. Edmund Gettier, "Is Justified True Belief Knowledge," *Analysis*, vol. 23 (1963), pp. 121–123.
4. For details see *The Stanford Encyclopedia of Philosophy*, art. "The Analysis of Knowledge" available on the internet, as well as the *Internet Encyclopedia of Philosophy*, art. "Gettier Problems."

Concept Dialectics in Historical Perspective

THE ROLE OF DISTINCTIONS

Distinctions enable the philosopher to remove inconsistencies not just by the brute negativism of thesis *rejection* but by the more subtle and constructive device of thesis *qualification*. The crux of a distinction is not mere negation or denial, but the amendment of an untenable thesis into something positive that does the job better. By way of example, consider the following aporetic cluster:

(1) All events are caused.
(2) If an action issues from free choice, then it is causally unconstrained.
(3) Free will exists—people can and do make and act upon free choices.

Clearly one way to exit from inconsistency is to abandon thesis (2). We might well, however, do this not by way of outright abandonment but rather by speaking of the "causally unconstrained" only in Spinoza's manner of *externally* originating casualty. For consider the result of deploying a distinction that divides the second premise into two parts:

(2.1) Actions based on free choice are unconstrained by *external* causes.
(2.2) Actions based on free choice are unconstrained by *internal* causes.

Once (2) is so divided, the initial inconsistent triad (1)–(3) give way to the quartet (1), (2.1), (2.2), (3). But we can resolve *this* aporetic cluster by rejecting (2.2) while yet retaining (2.1)—thus in effect *replacing* (2) by a weakened version. Such recourse to a distinction—here that between internal and external causes—makes it possible to avert the aporetic inconsistency and does so in a way that minimally disrupts the plausibility situation.

To examine the workings of this sort of process somewhat further, consider an aporetic cluster that set the stage for various theories of early Greek philosophy:

(1) Reality is one (homogeneous).
(2) Matter is real.
(3) Form is real.
(4) Matter and form are distinct sorts of things (heterogeneous).

In looking for a resolution here, one might consider rejecting (2). This could be done, however, not by simply *abandoning* it, but rather by *replacing* it—on the idealistic precedent of Zeno and Plato—with something along the following lines:

(2') Matter is not real as an independent mode of existence; rather it is merely quasi-real, a mere *phenomenon*, an appearance somehow grounded in immaterial reality.

The new quartet (1), (2'), (3), and (4) is entirely cotenable.

Now in adopting this resolution, one again resorts to a *distinction*, namely that between

i.   Strict reality as self-sufficiently independent existence

and

ii.   Derivative or attenuated reality as a (merely phenomenal) product of the operation of the unqualifiedly real.

Use of such a distinction between unqualified and phenomenal reality makes it possible to resolve an aporetic cluster—yet not by simply *abandoning* one of those paradox-engendering theses but rather by *qualifying* it. (Note, however, that once we follow Zeno and Plato in replacing (2) by (2')—and accordingly reinterpret matter as representing a "mere phenomenon"—the substance of thesis (4) is profoundly altered; the old contention can still be maintained, but it now gains a new significance in the light of new distinctions.)

Again one might—alternatively—abandon thesis (3). However, one would then presumably not simply adopt "form is not real" but rather would go over to the qualified contention that "form is not *independently* real; it is no more than a transitory (changeable) state of matter." And this can be looked at the other way around, as saying "form *is* (in a way) real, although only insofar as it is taken to be no more than a transitory state of matter." This, in effect, would be the position of the atomists, who incline to see as implausible any recourse to mechanisms outside the realm of the material.

Aporetic inconsistency can always be resolved in this way; we can always "save the phenomena"—that is, retain the crucial core of our various beliefs in the face of apparent consideration—by introducing suitable distinctions and qualifications. Once apory breaks out, we can thus salvage our philosophical commitments by *complicating* them, through revisions in the light of appropriate distinctions, rather than abandoning them altogether.

Consider the following aporetic cluster, which sets the stage for the traditional "problem of evil":

1. The world was created by God.
2. The world contains evil.
3. A creator is responsible for all defects of his creation.
4. God is not responsible for the evils of this world.

On this basis we have it that God, who by thesis 1 is responsible for all aspects of nature, is by 3 also responsible for evil. And this contradicts contention 4. To restore consistency, at least one of 1–4 must be abandoned. But now suppose that one introduces the distinction between *causal* responsibility and *moral* responsibility, holding that the causal responsibility of an agent does not necessarily entail a moral responsibility for the consequences of his acts. Then for *causal* responsibility, 3 is true but 4 false. And for *moral* responsibility, the reverse holds: 4 is true but 3 false. Once the distinction at issue is introduced, then no matter which way one turns on construing "responsibility," the inconsistency operative in the apory at issue is averted. Thus someone who adopts this distinction can retain *all* the aporetic theses—1 and 2 unproblematically and, as it were, half of each of 3 and 4—each in the sense of one side of the distinction at issue. The distinction enables us to make peace in the aporetic family at issue, by splitting certain aporetic theses into acceptable and unacceptable parts.

To be sure, distinctions are not needed if *all* that concerns us is averting inconsistency; simple thesis abandonment, mere refusal to assert, will suffice for that end. But distinctions are necessary if we are to maintain informative positions and provide answers to our questions. We can guard against inconsistency by avoiding commitment. But such skeptical refrainings leave us empty handed. Distinctions are the instruments we use in the (potentially never-ending) work of rescuing our assertoric commitments from inconsistency while yet salvaging what we can.

The history of philosophy is shot through with distinctions introduced to avert aporetic difficulties. Already in the dialogues of Plato, the first systematic writings in philosophy, we encounter distinctions at every turn. In Book I of the *Republic*, for example, Socrates' interlocutor quickly falls into the following apory:

1. Rational people always pursue their own interests.
2. Nothing that is in a person's interest can be disadvantageous to him.
3. Even rational people sometimes do things that prove disadvantageous.

Here, inconsistency is averted by distinguishing between two senses of the "interests" of a person—namely what is *actually* advantageous to him and what he merely *thinks* to be so, that is, between *real* and *seeming* interests. Again, in the discussion of "nonbeing" in the *Sophist*, the Eleatic stranger entraps Theaetetus in an inconsistency from which he endeavors to extricate himself by distinguishing between "nonbeing" in the sense of not existing *at all* and in the sense of not existing *in a certain mode*. For the most part, the Platonic dialogues present a dramatic unfolding of one distinction after another.

And this situation is typical in philosophy. The natural dialectic of problem solving here drives us even more deeply into drawing distinctions, so as to bring new, more sophisticated concepts upon the scene.

Whenever a particular aporetic thesis is rejected, the optimal course is not to abandon it altogether, but rather to minimize the loss by introducing a distinction by whose aid it may be retained *in part*. After all, we do have some commitment to the data that we reject, and are committed to saving as much as we can. (This, of course, is implicit in our treating those data as such in the first place.)

A distinction accordingly reflects a *concession*, an acknowledgment of some element of acceptability in the thesis that is being rejected. However, distinctions always bring a new concept upon the stage of consideration and thus put a new topic on the agenda. And they thereby present invitations to carry the discussion further, opening up new issues that were heretofore inaccessible. Distinctions are the doors through which philosophy moves on to new questions and problems. They bring new concepts and new theses to the fore.

DIALECTIC DEVELOPMENT VIA DISTINCTIONS

Distinctions enable us to implement the idea that a satisfactory resolution of aporetic clusters must somehow make room for all parties to the contradiction. The introduction of distinctions thus represents a Hegelian ascent—rising above the level of antagonistic positions to that of a "higher" conception, in which the opposites are reconciled. In introducing the qualifying distinction, we abandon the initial thesis and move toward its counterthesis, but we do so only by way of a duly hedged synthesis. In this regard, distinction is a "dialectical" process.

Philosophical distinctions are thus creative innovations. There is nothing routine or automatic about them—their discernment is an act of inventive ingenuity. They do not elaborate preexisting ideas but introduce new ones. They not only provide a basis for understanding better something heretofore grasped imperfectly but shift the discussion to a new level of sophistication and complexity. Thus, to some extent they "change the subject." (In this regard they are like the conceptual innovations of science which revise rather than explain prior ideas.)

Philosophy's recourse to ongoing conceptual refinement and innovation means that a philosophical position, doctrine, or system is never closed, finished, and complete. It is something organic, every growing and ever changing—a mere tendency that is in need of ongoing development. Its philosophical "position" is never actually that—it is inherently unstable, in need of further articulation and development. Philosophical systematization is a process whose elements develop in stages of interactive feedback—its exfoliation is a matter of dialectic, if you will.

Distinctions enable us to implement the irenic idea that a satisfactory resolution of aporetic clusters will generally involve a compromise that somehow makes room for all parties to the contradiction. The introduction of distinctions thus represents a Hegelian ascent—rising above the level of antagonistic doctrines to that of a "higher" conception, in which the opposites are reconciled. In introducing the qualifying distinction, we abandon that initial conflict-facilitating thesis and move toward its counterthesis—but only by way of a duly hedged synthesis. In this regard, distinction is a "dialectic" process. This role of distinctions is also connected with the thesis often designated as "Ramsey's Maxim." For with regard to disputes about fundamental questions that do not seem capable of a decisive settlement, Frank Plumpton Ramsey wrote: "In such cases it is a heuristic maxim that the truth lies not in one of the two disputed views but in some third possibility which has not yet been thought of, which we can only discover by rejecting something assumed as obvious by both the disputants."[1] On this view, then, distinctions provide for a higher synthesis of opposing views; they prevent thesis abandonment from being an *entirely* negative process, affording us a way of salvaging something, of giving credit where credit is due" even to those theses we ultimately reject. They make it possible to remove inconsistency not just by the brute force of thesis rejection, but by the more subtle and constructive device of thesis qualification.

The unfolding of distinctions accordingly plays a key role in philosophical inquiry because new concepts crop up in their wake so as to open up new territory for reflection. In the course of philosophy's dialectical development, new concepts and new theses come constantly to the fore and operate so as to open up new issues. And so in securing answers to our old questions we come to confront new questions that could not even be asked before.

The inherent dynamic of this dialectic deserves a closer look. Let us consider an historical example. The speculations of the early Ionian philosophers revolved about four theses:

(1) There is one single material substrate (*archê*) of all things.
(2) The material substrate must be capable of transforming into anything and everything (and thus specifically into each of the various elements).
(3) The only extant materials are the four material elements: earth (solid), water (liquid), air (gaseous), and fire (volatile)
(4) The four elements are independent—none gives rise to the rest.

Different thinkers proposed different ways out of this apory:

• Thales rejected (4) and opted for water as the *archê*.
• Anaximines rejected (4) and opted for air as the *archê*.
• Heraclitus rejected (4) and opted for fire as the *archê*.
• The Atomists rejected (4) and opted for earth as the *archê*.
• Anaximander rejected (3) and postulated an indeterminate *apeiron*.
• Empedocles rejected (1), and thus also (2), holding that everything consists in *mixtures* of the four elements.

Thus virtually all of the available exits from inconsistency were actually used. The thinkers involved either resolved to a distinction between genuinely primacy and merely derivative "elements" or, in the case of Empedocles, stressed the distinction between mixtures and transformation. But all of them addressed the same basic problem—albeit in the light of different plausibility appraisals.

As the Presocratics worked their way through the relevant ideas, the following conceptions (Figure 10.1) came to figure prominently on the agenda.

(I) $\left\{ \begin{array}{l} \text{(1) Whatever is ultimately real persists through change.} \\ \\ \text{(2) The four elements—earth (solid), water (liquid), air (gaseous), and fire} \\ \text{(volatile)—do not persist through change as such.} \\ \text{(3) The four elements encompass all there is by way of extant reality.} \end{array} \right.$

Figure 10.1

Three basic positions are now available:

(1)-abandonment: Nothing persists through change—*panta rhei*, all is in flux (Heraclitus).

(2)-abandonment: One single element persists through change—it alone is the *archê* of all things; all else is simply some altered form of it. This uniquely unchanging elements are: earth (atomists), water (Thales), and air (Anaximines). Or again, *all* the elements persist through change, which is only a matter of a variation in mix and proportion (Empedocles).

(3)-abandonment: Matter itself is not all there is—there is also its inherent geometrical structure (Pythagoras) or its external arrangement in an environing void (atomists). Or again, there is also an immaterial motive force that endows matter with motion—to wit, "mind" (*nous*) (Anaxagoras).

Let us follow along in the track of atomism by abandoning (3) though the distinction between material and nonmaterial existence. With this cycle of dialectical development completed, the following aporetic impasse (Figure 10.2) arose in pursuing the line of thought at issue:

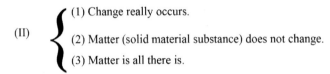

(II)
- (1) Change really occurs.
- (2) Matter (solid material substance) does not change.
- (3) Matter is all there is.

Figure 10.2

As always, different ways of escaping from contradiction are available:

(1)-abandonment: Change is an illusion (Parmenides, Zeno, Eleatics).
(2)-abandonment: Matter (indeed *everything*) changes (Heraclitus).
(3)-abandonment: Matter is not all there is; there is also the void—and the changing configurations of matter within it (atomism).

Taking up the third course, let us continue to follow the atomistic route. Note that this does not *just* call for abandoning (3), but also calls for sophisticating (2) to

(2') Matter as such is *not* changeable—it only changes in point of its variable rearrangements.

The distinction between *positional* changes and *compositional* changes comes to the fore here. This line of development has recourse to a "saving distinction" by introducing the new topic of variable configurations (as contrasted with such necessary and invariable states as the shapes of the atoms themselves).

To be sure, matters do not end here. A new cycle of inconsistency looms ahead. For this new topic paves the way for the following apory (Figure 10.3):

(III) $\Bigg\{$
(1) All possibilities of variation are actually realized.

(2) Various different world arrangements are possible.

(3) Only one world is real.

Figure 10.3

Again different resolutions are obviously available here:

(1)-rejection: A theory of real chance (*tuchê*) or contingency that sees various possibilities as going unrealized (Empedocles).
(2)-rejection: A doctrine of universal necessitation (the "block universe" of Parmenides).
(3)-rejection: A theory of many worlds (Democritus and atomism in general).

As the atomistic resolution represented by the second course was developed, apory broken out again:

(IV) $\Bigg\{$
(1) Matter as such never changes—the only change it admits of are its rearrangements.

(2) The nature of matter is indifferent to change. Its rearrangements are contingent and potentially variable.

(3) Its changes of condition are inherent in the (unchanging) nature of matter—they are necessary, not contingent.

Figure 10.4

Here the orthodox atomistic solution would lie in abandoning (3) and replacing it with

(3') Its changes of condition are not necessitated by the nature of matter. They are indeed quasi-necessitated by being law determined, but law is something independent of the nature of matter.

The distinction between internally necessitated changes and externally and accidentally imposed ones enters upon the scene. This resolution introduces a new theme, namely *law determination* (as introduced by the Stoics).

Yet when one seeks to apply this idea it seems plausible to add:
(V) (4) Certain material changes (contingencies, concomitant with free human actions) are not law determined

Apory now breaks out once more; the need for an exit from inconsistency again arises. And such an exit was afforded by (4)-abandonment, as with the law abrogation envisaged in the notorious "swerve" of Epicurus, or by (3')-abandonment, as with the more rigoristic atomism of Lucretius.

The developmental sequence from (I) through (V) represents an evolution of philosophical reflection through successive layers of aporetic inconsistency, duly separated from one another by successive distinctions. This process that led from the crude doctrines of Ionian theorists to the vastly more elaborate and sophisticated doctrines of later Greek atomism.

And this historical illustration indicates an important general principle. The continual introduction of the new ideas that arise in the wake of new distinctions means that the ground of philosophy is always shifting beneath our feet. And it is through distinctions that philosophy's prime mode of innovation—namely *conceptual* innovation—comes into play. And those novel distinctions for our concepts and contexts for our theses alter the very substance of the old theses. The dialectical exchange of objection and response constantly moves the discussion onto new—and increasingly sophisticated—ground. The resolution of antinomies through new distinctions is thus a matter of creative innovation whose outcome cannot be foreseen.

Concept auditing has in fact been one of the driving forces of philosophical development. For as the larger implications and ramifications of a particular concept come to be more widely contextualized and more deeply examined, it often becomes necessary to introduce distinction and electronics in whose absence problems and perplexities arose in earlier applications.

NOTE

1. Frank P. Ramsey, *The Foundations of Mathematics and Other Logical Essays*, ed. R. B. Braithwaite (London: K. Paul, Trench, Trubner & co., 1931), pp. 115–116.

#11

Metaphysical Illusions

When a financial audit is conducted, the detection of fraud is one of its possible outcomes. This sort of thing is also a possibility with concept audits.

An optical illusion occurs when we take ourselves to be seeing something that just is not there. A metaphysical illusion occurs when we take ourselves to be elucidating something that does not exist as such. Such an illusion can arise in metaphysics in the quest for an essence—a critically unifying X factor whose presumed co-presence throughout the items of a range of consideration is to unify these items into a single descriptive kind.

There are many illustrations of this, instanced by such questions as:

- What is intelligence—the shared factor that qualifies all intelligent beings as such?
- What is consciousness—the commonality of capacity that qualifies all conscious states and processes as such?
- What constitutes personal identity—the requisite commonalities that establish two otherwise described individuals as one and the same person?

The common presupposition of such questions is that there is an essential shared core that unifies the items at issue as instances of a certain sort.

The reality of it is that in such cases this presupposition is so questionable that is can safely be characterized as simply wrong. The questions at issue run afoul of a phenomenon that can be characterized as *contextual fragmentation*. Take personal identity and reidentification. Here different standards are clearly appropriate in different contexts: the legal for establishing claims of ownership or of restitution, the moral for justifying praise or blame, for dealing with relatives or friends, the biochemical for addressing inherited dispositions, etc.

51

Or take intelligence. There just is no single factor of intelligence that people do or do not have to a given extent. They have substantially differentiated capacities for verbal communication, arithmetical calculation, factual resolution, mechanical manipulation, etc.

And similar situations are obtained with respect to such metaphysically salient matters as consciousness, morality, causality, and numerous other issues. There simply is not essentially determinate common core here.

Take the idea of a *chair*. Who can say exactly what is and what a chair isn't and just what is it that qualifies an object to count as such. Obviously one can convey "the general idea," since otherwise this communicative item would be benefit of meaning. But precision is totally impracticable.

And this holds also for such abstract conceptions as that of *knowledge*. There just is no exactness to the idea of a person's knowing something. I have long known that Berlin is far away from Taipei. But until this very moment the thought never occurred to me. I know that people are presently astir in Kula Lampur, but no one ever informed me about it. I know that there are odd numbers bigger than a trillion, but yet have never bothered to think of any. No one has ever succeeded in spelling out the exact conditions under which it can truly and correctly be said that someone knows something.

Such examples illustrate a general point. Precision and exactness of detail is mechanical with respect to the terminology of ordinary-life communication in the language of everyday discourse. No definite boundary can be fixed here between the overall regions of appropriate and inappropriate application of the terms of reference at work there.

Only in legal contexts is a fair degree of conceptual precision achievable. Take adulthood. Some people are mature adults at 12, others have yet to get there at 20. But in matters of marrying, drinking, voting, making contracts, etc., the law injects an exactitude by arbitrary stipulation. Legal mandates and postulations dare to tread where the world's complexities input an imprecision.

What we have in everyday life—and philosophy as well—is a situation of where a certain conception is not geared to one stable determinative focus that fissions into a variety of facets linked by analogy and similarity in complexly related but significantly differentiated respects. The items at issue with such conceptions lack any common essential feature but only exhibit what Wittgenstein called a "family resemblance." The more closely we examine such ideas the more clearly there emerges the realization that what is at issue is not a coordinating uniformity of structure but a differentiated diversity. Even with something so seemingly simple as a "chair" or a "poem" there is really nothing that the items so characterized have in common over and above their shared characterization. Their conceptual integration lies entirely "in the minds of their beholders."

And the critical conceptual fallacy committed in such situations is one of what Kant called *hypostatization*, projecting a single shared factor (think here of "cause of cancer") when there is actually nothing but a diverse albeit analogous situations. Such proceeding creates out of "thin air," as it were, the conceptual mirage of a substantial core factor that simply is not there.

The point here is that those metaphysical notions predicated on an absent essential commonality are not well-defined concepts but misconceptions. Like the notion of "the cause of cancer" they are mistakenly predicted on the idea of a definite claim of commonality is at issue here in fact a varied plurality of complexity interrelated phenomena are at issue. And in such cases a properly conducted concept audit can reveal that what is at issue is not a well-defined concept but an illusion, so that where this inquiry sought for conceptual elucidation what actually results is concept-dissolution.

Different attunements to the different purposes of varying contexts of operation—functional efficacy in short—is the paramount consideration here. The sameness of "the same person," "the same poem," "the same ship," all function differently: there is no uniformity here. And even with one single such item—say "the same person" in relation to varying manifestations across space and time—there is contextual variation as between issues of legality, morality, affinity, and bio-medicine. And accordingly, concept auditing brings to view an indispensable need to keep due heed of conceptual differences.

Part III

FURTHER ILLUSTRATIVE APPLICATIONS

#12

Who Dun It?

The colonel was killed in the library with a heavy candlestick. Who did it? Identifying people and things can be a real problem, alike in cyberspace as in ordinary life.

What is it to identify someone? The English philosopher-logician J. O. Urmson had an answer: to single them out from everyone else. In a classic article "On Describing" he proposed that identification consist in providing an *uniquely applicable description*. On this basis we have identified an individual x in providing a description D that is applicable to this individual alone. Symbolically:

$$D x \,\&(\forall y)\,(Dy \rightarrow y = x)$$

There are, however, real problems here. Consider the problem of identifying the killer of that unfortunate colonel in the library. And let it be that our detective hero says: "I have managed to identify the killer: it was the person who wielded that candlestick at the time the colonel was killed." By the proposed standard he is quite right. He has indeed provided a uniquely applicable description (UAD) of the individual at issue. He has certainly *specified* that individual. But no one would concede that he has *identified* him. After all, we still don't have the least idea as to who that individual is.

The crux of the matter is that we have in view a number of standard ways for identifying people, such as

- by name, plus disambiguation when needed ("John Doe of 123 Maple Avenue," "Jane Doe, daughter of Tom and Betty Doe").
- by spatiotemporal location ("that man there [pointing]," The person just now entering the room").

57

- by unique role "The current president of France," "The king of England during WWI."

Only when the UAD at issue is one of a limited number of suitable kinds will we standardly accept the claim that an individual has actually been identified. Otherwise that UAD provides only for *specification* and not *identification*.

And much the same sort of thing when that issue on the agenda is one of specifying *which* rather than specifying *who*, and deals with objects rather than people. Thus consider the problem of identifying the bullet that killed the footman in the drawing room. It will obviously not do to say "The bullet that entered his skull just before he died." This UAD may be perfectly true, but it just does not do the job. To achieve the needed identification we would require something that proceeds along some more definitive route, such as

- by spatiotemporal location "that bullet there."
- the bullet depicted in the Exhibit A photograph

The lesson here is that item identification is something more complex and demanding than is at issue in Russell's barebones logical formula. Providing a uniquely applicable description (UAD) is not enough: it must be a description provided in a certain particular way. And what way is suitable is a matter of categorical dependency: it will say with the sort of thing at issue—be it a person, a physical object, or an immortal entity such as a corporation.

So with regard to item identity we once more have a situation where heed of the concept variations regarding the relevant ideas is required to keep matters on the right track.

#13

Existence

To Be Or Not To Be

ON BEING REAL

Metaphysics is traditionally characterized as the theory of being. But just what is it "to be"? What is at issue when we speak of being, existence, reality, and the like? Do philosophers in fact do justice to the actual use of these terms? A challenging problem arises in this area of conceptual audit.

On the surface of it, *to be* is to be an item that belongs to a well-defined realm of some sort. Such taxonomic kindhood is crucial for being because different sorts of things exist in very different ways. There is physical being in the order of space, time, and causality; mathematical being in the realm of quantities or structures; sensory being in the spectrum of colors or the manifold of odors; conceptual being in the realm of ideas; and so on. To be, in the most general sense of the term, is to play some part in such a realm of interrelated items, and there are as many modes of being as there are identifiable realms of meaningful deliberation.

Accordingly, the concept of *existence* is *syncategorematic* in the medieval logicians' sense of being applicable in various different categories. But this role and meaning in those different categories differs. But existing in space and time, as rocks do, is something very different from the sort of existence at issue with numbers or possibilities.

Since being is this realm-correlative, the idea at large is inherently contextualized. Strictly considered, then, we should not speak of existence or being categorically and without qualifications. For it is always a matter of being-as-something-or-other: as a physical object, as a number, as a shade of color, or the like. Being is accordingly not homogeneous and universal but categorically differentiated: different kinds of items are beings in their own type-characteristic way. To attribute to numbers the same kind of being that

59

colors or that mammals have would be to commit a serious category mistake that invites incomprehension.

This said, however, it should also be acknowledged that in philosophical deliberation the most central and salient mode of existence is being as a concrete object in the real world as part of the observable furnishings of the physical universe.

For sure, figuring in the world's causal commerce will indeed qualify something as unquestionably existing. But where are we to move on from here?

The fact of it is that existence is best characterized recursively. We would thus begin with the straightforward existence of things in space and time in the manner of trees, dogs, and automobiles. And we then thus proceed reiteratively somewhat as follows, specifying that something exists if

1. It exists unproblematically in the just-specified manner of playing an active causal role in this real world of ours.
2. It is something whose actual existence must be invoked in providing a satisfactory explanatory account of the features of something that exists. (And here it does not matter if the explanatory account at issue is efficiently causal, or functionally finalistic, or conceptually explicative.)

Such a definition is essentially recursive, maintaining first that ordinary material objects are existentially real, and thereupon extending this stepwise to anything whatsoever that is bound up with the existent by way of explanatory linkages—such linkages being causal in the first order, and expository in the second. It is clear, however, that this specification rejects the Eleatic Principle that a thing must have causal power to be real. For this would rule out the existence of abstracta which claims of the position explicitly brought into the arena of consideration. And a liberal approach to the matter will also be prepared to admit as real those things whose acceptance as real facilitates the project of understanding—anything whose assumed existence figures in our best-available explanation of the real. Thus not observation alone but conception too can be seen to qualify in suitable circumstances as a viable cognitive pathway to existence. And on this basis abstracta (such as colors and textures) and mathematica (such as numbers and shapes) can be accredited with an existence of sorts.

But there are limits to what can be achieved in this way. Philosophers have devised technical expressions such as "to subsist" and the like to stand for contextualized "existence" within the fictional realm at issue with assumptions, suppositions, hypotheses, and literary fictions. Should we say that Sherlock Holmes quasi-exits in reality because he "exists" in the Conan Doyle stories? This seems a questionable usage because such items are, by hypothesis, no more than mere thought-things and so the issue arises of how much ontological weight such supposed quasi-being can bear.

And so, in reflecting a real thing we come to realize that there are actually two sorts of being; namely

- *actual existence* in the realm of space, time, and physical process
- *hypothetical being* in some domain of thought or dissuasion (in a work of fiction, in a domain of numbers, in a person's imagination, etc.)

So besides existence in the real (or "natural") world, there is also domain-relative being in a specifiable domain of deliberation.

All the same, the only sort of quasi-reality or quasi-existence which something that is a mere (nonfactual) possibility ever has is that which it acquires in the framework of discourse and discussion. Its being consists in being thinkable. (Following this view of the matter might be called *fictionalism*, to borrow a term from D. M. Armstrong.[1]) On this perspective, fictions "subsist" in the realm of supposition or hypothesis, and here alone. And the crucial fact is that objects of discussion are no more authentic objects than hobby horses are horses or tin soldiers are soldiers. (To *call* something an *X* does not make it an *X*! Verbal legerdemain creates only claims and statements but not objects of a different sort.) And figuring in works of fiction and imagination does not suffice to establish a claim upon being as more strictly understood. Since to be is to function on one's own—to have a footing as a constituent of a thought-independent realm and play some self-subsistingly functional role in a domain of interrelated items of some sort—it will not do to say "To be is to be thought of—to be an object of consideration." Being thought about, talked about, imagined is not to take part in an independent realm of one's own but simply to figure in the ideas of some mind or other, and this does not suffice for the self-sufficiency needed to ratify a claim to existence.

The well-known logician's dictum "to be is to be the value of a (symbolic) variable" is not much help in matters of ontology. For "to be" in *this* sense is simply to be an object of discussion, since we will—or certainly can—put anything we care to discuss into the domain of discourse at issue with our variables. (After all, one can quantify over the character of Shakespeare's comedies without ascribing actual existence to Puck and Ganymede.) To "exist" as a character in fiction is not to *exist* at all, although this is a matter of metaphysical conscientiousness, not of logical principle. Such things do not exist; such being as they have they possess by being hypothetical and functioning as thought-objects.

Construing existence in the decidedly liberal presently contemplated goes beyond the doctrinal stance that D. M. Armstrong calls *naturalism*: the position that the only objects that exist are those physically constituting this real world of ours. This partitive or mereological realism is simply too restrictive. For as the present, decidedly more liberal account sees it, there exist not only *parts* of existing objects but also items that are merely features of them— realty-characterizing features as items such as properties, relationships, force-fields, etc. And while these do not themselves constitute objects in the world, they too can stake a claim or existence—albeit only insofar as they do or can serve to account for some features of the world's objects.

This distinction emerges straightforwardly in the conceptual reconstruction of the vocabulary range of existence, being, reality, fiction, conceivably, etc. And it is important to bear it in mind in philosophical deliberations. For of course the being of shapes and of ideas are very different things. To treat such answers as equivalent is to commit a serious category mistake.

A judicious mode of realism will tread with caution over a middle ground with regard to being. If it conducts its concept auditing with due care, it will neither flatly deny being to things which—like fictions—do not exist in the physical domain, nor yet incline to ascribe to them the same sort of being that physical objects indeed have. As a concept audit of the relevant ideas shows, different sorts of things are plausibly said to have being, but they will inevitably do so in their own way or fashion. In this respect the existence of uniform commonalities will be purely coincidental.[2]

IDENTIFICATION ISSUES

There are infinitely many integers. But there are only finitely many occasions (albeit a great many of them) when humans refer to this or that particular one of them. Given the situation, there have to be unmentioned integers. And therefore one of them has to be the first, the smallest in the count order of 1, 2, 3, ... But of course one cannot possibly identify it since doing so would be self-defeating. This smallest unnamed number is veiled in a cloud of unknowing. No one can possibly identify it. It is seemingly unidentifiable.

On a smaller scale, suppose that a group of people are playing Musical Chairs. We know that one of them will remain unseated after the music stops. And we know that it has to be one of this limited group. But we cannot as yet possibly identify this individual. Again, "the person who remains unseated when the music stops" is veiled in a cloud of unknowing. No one can possibly (as yet) identify this individual. It is someone seemingly unidentifiable.

This puzzle of the nameless integer and the unidentifiable Musical Chairs player brings to light that identification-incapacity is an inherently equivocal conception that admits of two decidedly distinct constructions.

In Construction I we have it that:

- It is not the case that every member of the group can possibly be identified (or seated): someone is necessarily unidentifiable:

$$\sim(\forall x)\Diamond Ix \text{ or equivalently } (\exists x)\square\sim Ix$$

By contrast, in Construction II we have it that:

- It is not possible that every member of the group can be identified (or seated)

$$\sim\Diamond(\forall x)Ix \text{ or equivalently } \square(\exists x)\sim Ix$$

As the symbolic formulation makes patently clear, two rather different conditions are at issue, and they bring to light two very different senses of an infeasibility of identification/seating. Alike with number identification and Musical Chairs we have unidentifiability only in Sense II and not in Sense I.

And then there is once again the issue of being. A widely accepted precept has it that identification is a prerequisite for being. But being does not—should not—require actual identification; it should reach no further than in-principle identifiability. Here too one must resort to a needed distinction.

The salient point is that in neither case is there any identifiable individual who cannot possibly be identified/seated—no one for whom this accommodation is in principle impossible. And this situation is not without its philosophical implications. Consider just one example. Aristotle proposed construing the impossible as that which never happens. The present analysis suggests that this idea simply does not work. There will be integers that will never be identified but no one integer is, in principle, unindentifiable.)

NOTES

1. D. M. Armstrong, *A Combinatorial Theory of Possibility* (Cambridge: Cambridge University Press, 1989).

2. This conclusion that being/existence is not univocal but involves a merely analogical unity of conception was among the principal teachings of the Spanish neo-Scholastic Francisco Suarez (1548–1617). (See especially the second of his *Metaphysical Disputations*, first published in two volumes in 1597.)

#14

Explanatory Regression

INFINITE REGRESSION

Some philosophers envision a regressively ancestral determinism where any causally determined action is in turn determined by an earlier one until at least the action is determined by circumstances that pre-exist the agent and thereby obviously fail to be under his control.[1] But there is a big problem here. For deliberations regarding free will are all too often vitiated by what one might call the Zenonic Fallacy. It emerges in the following line of reasoning:

> If every action is determinately fixed in place by the laws of nature and temporally antecedent events, then the chain of causality can be carried back into the distant past.

This Zenonic Fallacy is exemplified in the reasoning which Daniel Dennett formulates on the following terms:

> If determinism is true, then our every deed and decision is the inexorable outcome, it seems, of the sum of physical forces acting at the moment; which in turn is the inexorable outcome of the forces acting an instant before, *and so on to the beginning of time* .... [Thus]—If determinism is true, then our acts are the consequences of the laws of nature and events in the remote past. But it is not up to us what went on before we were born, and neither is it up to us what the laws of nature are. Therefore the consequences of these things (including our present acts) are not up to us.[2]

It is exactly in this italicized transit from "and so on" to "the beginning of time" that constitutes what I shall call the Zenonic Fallacy. And fallacy it is, because it overlooks the prospect of backwards convergence, drawing ever closer to a fixed prior terminus, but never passing it.[3]

After all, it is exactly in this transit from "and so on" to "the beginning of time" that the Zenonic Fallacy consists. For the reasoning at issue overlooks the prospect of backwards *convergence* as illustrated Figure 14.1.

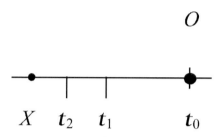

Figure 14.1

Assume an occurrence O at t_0—the result, so we suppose, of a free decision at X and suppose a time sequence of t_i with t_{i+1} standing halfway between X and t_i. And now consider the following situation. Everything at O can be explained causally via events during the interval t_1–t_0 and everything at t_1 can be explained causally via events during the interval t_2–t_1, and so on ad infinitum along an unendingly compressed chain of causation. So *every* event from X to O can in fact be explained causally. But there is now no obstacle to the prospect that *nothing* in this chain can be explained causally via events occurring *antecedently* to X, the juncture at which a free decision occurs. And this sort of causal compression is fatal to any "and-so-on" retrogression into the distant past.

So it is simply false that because our present acts are causal consequences of what goes before they must arise from the state of things in the distant past—matters over which we obviously have no control, thus leaving no room for free will.[4] The key point here is that a compressive backward convergence can finalize retrogression. Overlooking this key point is the heart and core of the Zenonic Fallacy.

Zeno's notorious paradox of Achilles and the tortoise led to the conclusion that even an infinite number of steps forward cannot cover a small distance. The Zenonic Fallacy has it that an infinite number of backwards steps must cover a great distance. And this latter argument overlooks the fact that, thanks to convergence, an infinity of summands can yield a finite sum, provided merely that the steps get ever shorter. In Zeno's argument, Achilles never catches the tortoise because his progress must go on and on before the endpoint is reached. In the present reasoning explanation will never reach an initiating choice-point because the regress goes on and on ever further. But in both cases alike the idea of a convergence which terminated the infinite process at issue after a finite timespan is simply ignored. The analysis of

Zeno's paradox carries exactly this lesson: An infinite succession of steps need not cover an infinite distance. So, once it is granted that, even if a cause must precede its effect, nevertheless there is no specific timespan, however small, by which it need do so, the causal regression argument against free will loses all of its traction. A causal determinism of actions is then perfectly compatible with a causal freedom with respect to decisions and choices.

Surprisingly, it seems somehow to have eluded numerous theorists that it is perfectly possible to have a causal chain tracing back ad infinitum, but nevertheless converging on a point of closure only a finite time in the past.

ACCOMPLISHMENTS VERSUS ACTIONS

In matters of temporal regression it proves useful to distinguish between an agent's accomplishments and his actions. An accomplishment is a result that the agent manages to achieve, whereas an action is a performance that is done wittingly and intentionally with conscious awareness of what one is doing—something in which the agent's attention and intention is involved. When I stretch my muscles in arising in the morning, I achieve on accomplishment, but do not perform an action, seeing that what I (generally) do proceeds below the threshold of deliberate awareness.

Now the crucial point for present purposes is that accomplishments are time-compressible. When I move my finger from point A to point B, I make a multitude of motions. But of course they then lie below the radar screen of conscious awareness and intention—if only in view of their temporal brevity. They are accomplishments but not actions. Actions, by contrast, are not time-compressible. There is some minimal period of time—possibly differing from individual to individual—for deploying the conscious attention needed to make a performance into an actual action.

Now the crucial point for present purposes is that *any regress that requires the realization of an infinitude of actions is thereby vicious*, seeing that the following contentions involve us in logical inconsistency

- X's accomplishments involve an infinite regress of actions
- X's accomplishments can be realized within a finite timespan
  Consider in this light the difference between
- For an occurrence to be realized, there must also occur the immediate causes that engender it.

  and

- To *explain* an occurrence adequately, one must also *explain* the occurrence of the immediate causes that engender it.

In the first case we have a regress alright, but in the end it is simply a descriptive feature of the manifold of productive causality, turning on an aspect of its infinitely complex causal network. There is no vitiating problem about this, and no reason of principle why this regress should be unrealizable and problematic. But the second case is something else again. For it bears upon our actions in a way that projects an infinite series of *performatory preconditions* whose vitiating regress defeats the very idea of adequate explanation.

And exactly the same situation is at issue with the difference between saying:

• Every proposition admits of a demonstration when it is true

and saying

• Every proposition requires a demonstration to be acceptable as true

The first thesis is an innocuous analytical observation about the inferential structure of the domain of truth. The second, by contrast, absurdly posits an unrealizable productive standard for truth-acceptance. It relates not to what is but to what must be done to bring something to be. In one case, we begin with a *given* reality and subjects it to analytically regressive treatment. But in the other case one resorts to a synthetic regress in unavoidably futile endeavor to realize performatively some particular results.

PRE-CONDITIONS VERSUS CONSEQUENCES AND CO-CONDITIONS

Some writers[5] deliberate about regress in the light of the "truth regress" engendered by the Tarski Equivalence for truth:

$$(T)p \text{ if and only if: '}p\text{' is true.}$$

As a general principle, this launches into the (clearly endless) recursive regress based on the regression rule:

$$\text{'}p\text{' is true} \rightarrow p$$

On this basis, skeptically minded theorists incline to argue that to claim p, you must have it that 'p' is true, and this in turn can only be achieved if you have "'p' is true" is true, and so on down the line. But this overlooks a critically important point. For the regress at issue can be looked at two decidedly different ways: consequential and preconditional. When "'*p*' is true" is taken as an inferential *consequence* of *p*, this sets afoot an infinite analytical regression that is essentially harmless. Only if establishing "*p* is true" were seen as an epistemic *precondition* for the assertability of *p*, would we be launched into a vicious and vitiating regression that would demolish any prospect of warranted assertability. With that link seen as a relationship of *consequence* there is no problem; only when seen as a relationship of *precondition* will there be difficulty.

Consider such conditions as

- To justify a claim to facticity, one must be able to justify the grounds on which this claiming is based.
- To know a fact securely, one must securely know the facts that ground it in providing the reasons of its acceptance.
- To define a term in a fully satisfactory way, one must define the terms used in its definition.

These claims all provide the launching platform for a infinite cyclic regress.

However, there are two ways of construing the "one must" at issue in these contentions. One is to read it as a *pre-condition*: "one must *first and in advance*." The other is as a *co-condition*: "one must *ultimately be in a position to*." It is clear that in the first reading the regress is vicious and vitiating. But in the second reading it is unproblematic and harmless.

Thus consider the contention: "To understand a proposition adequately one must first understand the question(s) it is designed to answer. And to understand a question adequately one must first understand the propositions that constitute its presuppositions." Here we have a regression of demands that are clearly vicious in its Catch-23 aspect of eliminating from the very outset any prospect of adequate understanding.

Which came first, the chicken or the chicken egg? Are we not plunged into an endless regress here? After all, it takes chickens to produce chicken eggs and chicken eggs to produce chickens. But viewed in a deeper perspective we are dealing not so much with things (chickens and eggs) but with concepts. And here, at the conceptual level, there is in fact co-emergence. For until the evolutionary development of chicken has reached a certain stage, one would not *call* these creatures chickens, and thus would not *call* those productions chicken eggs. Seen in this light, chickens and chicken eggs came upon the scene conjointly and together. We have a situation of *conceptual co-emergence*. And so when asked "What comes first, the chicken or the chicken-egg?" the appropriate answer is: *neither*—they came upon the scene conjointly and concurrently whenever it was that there came upon the scene the sort of things one would be prepared to characterize as chickens. The crux is coordination. The problem of infinite regress does not arise here because the real issue before us is one of conceptual coordination rather than productive priority.

Thomas Hobbes insisted the human will itself does not function voluntarily. He reasoned as follows:

> The will is not voluntary. For a man can no more way that he will will, than that he will will will, and so to make an infinite repetition of the word will, which is absurd and insignificant.[6]

Here the common confusion between *preconditions* and *consequences* is once more at work. For there is a crucial difference saying that when a man wills he must, in order to do so, *first* will so to will, and between saying that when a man wills he *thereby also* wills so will. However, the long and short of it is that this supposed regress of willings is an illusion. No sorts of preconditions are at work here. Or put differently, the idea that willing to will is yet another further act of willing is an illusion. That "willing to will" is simply an integral part of the willing itself.[7] We are once again dealing with coordination and not prerequisites.

CONCLUSION

Infinite regression is certainly not vicious as such. Various distinctions can come into operation to render it harmless. In particular, the difference between vicious and innocuous regression is marked by a variety of crucial distinctions: specifically those between

- regressive limitation as against unlimitedness and specifically between nonconvergent regress and the limited regress of compressive convergence.
- infinite true-to-type regression as against regression into obscurity.
- infinite regresses that are co-requisite or even consequential as against those that are actually presuppositional.
- infinite regresses that are compositionally structural as against those that are performatory.
- realized accomplishments as against unachievable performances.

As unendingly infinite regress will be innocuous when
- regresses that inappropriately treat item as *preconditions* as against those that should properly be seen as *co*-conditions or *consequences*.

And so, overall, a clear lesson emerges. Infinite regress is not something that is absurd as such, involving by its very nature a fault or failing that can be condemned across the board. Its viciousness will depend on the specifics of the case. And here a cluster of important distinctions function so as to separate the sheep of regressive harmlessness from the regressively vicious goats.

NOTES

1. See, for example, Lehrer 1974.

2. Dennett, *Elbow Room: The Varieties of Free Will Worth Wanting* (Cambridge: MIT Press, 1984), p. 99 (my italics). Compare also ibid, p. 134 and Dennett, *Freedom Evolves* (New York: Viking, 2003), p. 16.

3. To illustrate "backward convergence" think of retreating to point 1 from point 2, and does so by successive halfway steps, first to the midpoint between 1 and 2, then to the midpoint from there to 2, and so on. With each step one draws closer to point 2, but will never succeed in reaching it.

4. See Carl Ginet, "Infinitism is not the Solution to the Regress Problem," in Matthias Setup (ed.), *Contemporary Debates in Epistemology* (Malden, MA: Blackwell Publishing, 2005), pp. 140–149.

5. See, for example, Daniel Nolan, "What's Wrong with Infinite Regresses?" *Metaphilosophy*, vol. 32 (2001), pp. 523–538.

6. Thomas Hobbes, *The Elements of Law Natural and Political and Human Nature*, chap 12, par 5, ed. by J. C. A. Gaskin (New York: Oxford University Press, 1994).

7. For other approaches to addressing Hobbes' regress of conditions, see Yeomans 2006.

#15

The Fallacy of Respect Neglect

RESPECT NEGLECT

What is here characterized as The Fallacy of Respect Neglect is particularly common error among philosophers. It is a prominent instance of the broader Fallacy of Illicit Amalgamation which consists in treating as a single uniform unit something that in fact involves a diversified plurality of separate issues. Specifically it has the form of treating a feature F as an unified property that things do or do not have, where in fact F is a matter of various respects, so that things can have F in one respect and lack it in another. There are many instances of this phenomenon, for example the *simplicity* of scientific theories, the *preferability* of objects of choice, the *goodness* of persons, the *fairness* of decision processes, and many others.

Clearly, some features of things are monolithic and categorical, a matter of yes/no and on/off. And act is either legal or not, a task either feasible or not. But, equally clearly, this is not always the situation that prevails. Many features disaggregate into respects.

Some features are maxi-respectival: To have F you must have it in *all* respects: if something fails to be F in a single respect, then it is not F at all. Perfection is like that, as is the justice of an action—or its legality or its honesty or its courtesy.

Other features are mini-perspectival: To have F it suffices to have it in *some* respects: if something has F in even a single respect, then it has F flat-out. Imperfection and injustice like that, as is the generosity of an act or its foolishness.

It is easy to see that in denying features that are maxi-perspectival or in ascribing features that are mini-perspectival, we can give respects a short shift

71

because one single case suffices. But of course not all features will be like that. And this is particularly so in the case of evaluative features.

To be sure, it may also happen that there is respectival dominance where one single factor is by itself all-determinative. In the case of safety, survivability-geared safety from destruction will be an example: If we do not survive in the short run there is no use worrying about matters further down the road. But it is not easy to think of other examples of this sort where one single respect-dimension is all-out predominant and thereby able to speak for the totality, so that a proliferation of respects does not come into it. But many important features of things are neither mini- nor maxi-perspectival. And here the proliferation of respects becomes critical. And the fallacy of respect-neglect arises when this critical consideration is ignored, as it so often is in matters of evaluation.

Let us consider some examples.

SIMPLICITY AS AN ILLUSTRATION

Simplicity has certainly played a prominent role in twentieth century philosophy of science—especially in methodologically governed discussions of reductive reasoning. From C. S. Peirce to Rudolf Carnap and Hans Reichenbach and beyond, philosophers of science have seen the simplicity of theories as a key factor for their acceptability.

All the same, it is clear on even casual inspection that the idea of simplicity in relation to theories splits apart into a proliferation of respects:

- *expressive simplicity*: syntactical economy in the machinery of formulation.
- *conceptual simplicity*: semantical economy of exposition, avoidance of complex ideas and presuppositions that require elaborate explanation.
- *instrumental simplicity*: in terms of the amount of mathematical apparatus needed for formulating the theory (mere algebra, calculus, complex function theory, etc.)
- *computational simplicity*: how easy it is to compute results and outcomes by use of the theory,
- *pedagogical simplicity*: how easy it is to teach the theory and to learn it.

The salient point here is that we here encounter a diversified manifold of perspectives of consideration from which one theory can be seen as simpler than another.

It is an important consideration that these different modes of simplicity are not necessarily in agreement. Consider an analogy: the simplicity of automobiles. One can be simpler than another in point of

- being easier to manufacture
- being easier to maintain
- being easier to start
- being easier to drive

And these can and actually do conflict with one another. A car that is easier/simpler to manufacture is not necessarily one that is easier/simpler to drive. Moreover, even these factors themselves proliferate further. The "easier to drive" will split apart into "in dry conditions," "in wet conditions," "on smooth and well maintained roads," etc. With automobiles simplicity is critically respectival. And the simplicity of theories is in much the same boat.

To say that one object—be it a theory, an auto, an action, idea, belief, or whatever—is simpler than another is perfectly proper and meaningful—but only if one specifies some particular respect or aspect. Here one cannot appropriately speak of simplicity *tout court*. And to fail to acknowledge that simplicity is subject to fission into a plurality of respects that may potentially even conflict with one another is to succumb to what might be characterized as the Fallacy of Respect Neglect.

It would be futile to seek to escape the Fallacy of Respect Neglect by seeking to have it that *real* simplicity is a matter of being simpler in *every* respect, so that respectivization becomes irrelevant. But this is all too often decidedly impracticable. But of course, whenever different respects are mutually conflicting—as we see in the automobile example—there will be no workable way of taking this step. And this situation is only too common.

FURTHER EXAMPLES

Political theorists of democratic inclination often maintain that in matters of social decision the preferability of alternatives is to be decided by the choices of individuals. Philosophers of science maintain that in matters of theory choice the preferability of alternatives is to be decided by the explanatory merit of theories. But the eligibility of items from the standpoint of individuals may well be (and all too often is) a matter of respect with A being preferred to B in one regard and B to A in another—and neither respect predominating over the other. And the explanatory merit of theories in one regard (e.g., generality) and range of applicability may be at odds with its explanatory merit in another (such as ease of application).

Merit and preferability in all applications of their idea are matters of respect. Take something as simple as a house. Clearly one may be superior to another in part of location, roominess, circulation, solidity, etc. And this sort of situation obtains with matters of social policy as well.

Take equality—another theme that is currently popular with political theorists. Equality can be a matter of opportunity, of access, of regard, of treatment of shares in the distribution of goods and bads, etc. And here too there can be conflicts. In giving each holder of a lottery ticket an equal chance at the whole prize we preclude their sharing it equally.

Again take the idea—popular with some philosophers of science—that scientific theories "are equivalent when they have the same mathematical structure." This could perhaps be made to work if the idea of structure were a respect-free: monolith rather than respectival. But just as a sentence expressed in language has a grammatical structure, a lexicographic structure, a thematic structure, a rhythmic structure, etc. so a scientific theory has many sorts of structure. And indeed even a given mathematical fact can find its expression in ways that differ substantially in structure. (The structure of the expression of the fact that two plus two is four is very different in the arithmetic of *Principia Mathematica* and in its formulation by Goedelian means. And conversely, a single "structurally identical" formula can acquire very different meanings in different contexts, e.g., in binary and decimal arithmetic.)

Hermeneutic theorists occasionally embark on the quest for correct interpretation. But clearly the real question is not "Is there a single right interpretation?" as per a recent book of that title.[1] For to ask if there is one single right interpretation (of a literary or philosophical text, a painting, etc.) is to invite the Fallacy of Respect Neglect. To pose a genuinely meaningful question one would have to ask "Is there one single interpretation that is optimal in a certain particular specified respect." And here the correct answer is that rather uninteresting response—sometimes Yes and sometimes No. After all, that original question is muddled through the fact that interpretations have different aspects, different respects. Interpretation can be geared to the intentions of the author, to the general understandings and expectations of the audience, to the issue of utility for our own problems, and so on. And it is effectively impossible—in principle as in practice—that one single interpretation can be right or optimal in every respect.

Such deliberations point to a general conclusion. Committing the Fallacy to Respect Neglect invites unhappy consequences—confusion if not outright self-contradiction. And this is not only in the case of the particular issue that presently concerns us—such as simplicity—but is a whole host of other cases as will (preferability, similarity, utility, predictability, importance, testability, etc.).

PERSPECTIVAL DISSONANCE AND NON-AMALGAMATION

It might be thought that respective fusion or amalgamation is the cure for respect-proliferation. It is not. Thus suppose some positivity or negativity is to be allocated among several equally deserving parties. Then there is

- fairness of opportunity
- fairness of result
- fairness of process

In point of result it seems unfair to allocate the entire item to X rather than Y. But if this was determined by a spin of the roulette wheel then there was fairness of opportunity. On the other hand, if the good was divisible and could have been shared out in equal portions then it processualy unfair to allocate it by lot. But of course the case of indivisible goods shows that one cannot reply that (categorical) fairness is simply of being fair in every respect, seeing that here realizing fairness in one respect may preclude the prospect of realizing it in another.

Whenever a higher-level factor of desirability—such as that of simplicity or economy or convenience—fissions into a plurality of different respects or aspects these will often—perhaps even generally—prove to be combination-resistant. Consider the analogy of ease and convenience in the context of food. This is clearly something that is subject to respect-proliferation:

- easier to produce
- easier to prepare
- easier to digest
- easier to acquire

A food that is easy to prepare for eating (e.g., a ripe banana)—will not be easier to come by if we don't live in a banana-growing region. A food may well need more complicated preparation (e.g., cooking) if it is to be easier to digest, etc., there is no way in which one food can be easier overall than another because the various respects of ease may be—and indeed are—in conflict with one another.

And just the same sort of situation is going to obtain in the case of such concepts as similarity or preferability or the like. All of them dissolve into a plurality of respects which will themselves have yet further respects. And—most relevantly for our present purposes—this is going to hold for simplicity as well. For most any respect-involving notion like those just mentioned is going to be inherently diversified, subject to different aspects that cannot simply be forced together in smooth coordination because more of one of them will be obtainable only at the price of less of another.

And this internal diversity stands in the way of amalgamation even as the inner tension among the various rational aspects of simplicity precludes one thing's being simpler than another in every potentially relevant respect. There will be no way of fusing the different aspects into one unified overall result. For seeing that the simplicity—in our present case—is inherently respect-localized it fails to admit a global, symphatically unified version. There will be simplicity (or preferability, or similarity, etc.) in this or that respect, but no such thing as an all-in, unrestrictedly global realization of the idea. And to insist on overlooking those manifold discordant respects is to prelude the realization of anything meaningful. The complex realities of the case block the prospect of integrative fusion, of overall unification.

The fallacy of respect neglect leads to another philosophical pitfall, that of what might be called a *desideratum perplex*. This arises when things can be desirable in many different respects which unfortunately, however, cannot all be combined at once, even as a house that is large enough for extensive entertaining will not be small enough for ease and economy in matters of cleaning and maintenance.

There are various vivid illustrations of this in recent philosophically significant contexts. One relates to what is called the "Arrow Paradox" in matters of economic rationality. In his Nobel Prize-winning work of the 1950s, Kenneth Arrow was able to show that in their pursuit of economic optimality, the aficionados of preference-based welfare economics had projected a manifold of idealized desiderata which (in the very logic of the situation) just were not conjointly satisfiable.

A further illustration of this phenomenon arises in relation to what might be called Milnor's Paradox in the theory of economic rationality. When an individual faces problems of choice in conditions of uncertainty, there are various standards of rational choice, each looking to the matter from the angle of a different aspect of desirability. But here, once again, as John Milnor showed in 1954, conjoint realization of these different aspects of desirability is a logicomathematical impossibility.[2]

As such cases illustrate, if one ignores the potential conflicts among respects of desirability and simply operates with an uncritical amalgam in which diverse aspect of desirability are run together, one may well have an unrealizable impracticability on one's hands.

SUMMARY

The fallaciousness of respect neglect roots in the fact that we cannot in general make absolutes out of comparatives. One leaf may be greener than another, but there is no such thing as anything absolutely and utterly green. One book may be harder than another but there is no such thing as an absolutely and totally hard book. One route may be easier than another, but there is no such thing as an absolutely or totally easy route. Against this background the move from comparative to absolute simplicity—or equality, or preferability, etc.— becomes deeply problematic.

Nor can we generally make categoricals out of respectivals. A sentence may be awkward in this or that respect but it cannot be unrestrictedly awkward. A tool may be useful in this or that respect, but it cannot be unqualifiedly useful. And even so, one thing can be simpler than another in this or that respect, but it is not only will not but cannot be categorically (unrestrictedly, unqualifiedly, and unavoidably) simple.

The long and short of it is that respect neglect is a common pitfall in philosophical deliberations. And when matters stand one way when something obtains in one respect and not in another, then (as Aristotle already insisted[3]) in neglecting respects and riding roughshod over the differences involved, we all too readily fall into contradiction and thereby become unable to do that to which philosophers must always aspire: talking good sense.[4]

NOTES

1. See *Is There a Single Right Interpretation*, ed. by Michael Krausz (University Park, PA: Pennsylvania State University Press, 2002).

2. On these issues see Paul Diesing, *Science and Ideology in the Policy Sciences* (New York: Aldine, 1982), pp. 44–47.

3. Aristotle, *Metaphysics* III2996b28ff; *On Interpretation* VI, 17a33ff. On the issues see R. M. Dancy, *Sense and Contradiction: A Study in Aristotle* (Dordrecht: D. Reidel, 1975).

4. This chapter is a revision of an article of the same title published in *Philosophy and Phenomenological Research*, vol. 71 (2005), pp. 392–398.

Appearance and Reality

CLARIFYING A DISTINCTION

Considerable mischief has been done in philosophy by misunderstanding the distinction between appearance and reality at issue in the classical specifications:

appearance = how things are thought to be

reality = how things actually are

All too commonly philosophers have transmuted such a *conceptual distinction* into a *substantial separation* and mistakenly made the shift from thinking of things differently to what is actually something quite another thing, namely thinking of different things. For of course distinct matters are at issue here. When I think of you as the musician next door and as the local banker I am not dealing with different people but only with different ways of considering one selfsame individual. This is in every bit as flawed as would be the idea that distinguishing between musicians and bankers conceptually means that someone of the one sort could not also belong to the other—that a banker could not possibly be a musician as well. It is a mistaken idea that is conceptually *distinct* is ipso facto also substantively *disjoint*.

And this holds in the present context as well. Thus consider "that chair over there" (pointing) and "the one and only real chair in the room." In theory these could be very different things, but in fact they are not. Different conceptualizations need not result in different referents. It is emphatically not the case that knowledge of reality is in principle infeasible because reality is somehow a *Ding an sich*, a Kantian "thing in itself" hidden away behind the "veil of

78

appearance." Reality is—at least in part—something that stands before that "veil," identical with that which happens to be accurate and correct. For the actuality of it is that things sometimes—perhaps even frequently—are exactly as they appear to be, there is nothing which in principle stands in the way.

In such matters the paramount contrast—or should be—is that between how things are *correctly* thought to be and how they are *erroneously* thought. These indeed can never be the same, unlike what *is* and what *is thought to be*. The salient distinction is accordingly that not that between mere belief and actual fact, but that between belief that is true (correct) and that which is not.

FROM APPEARANCE TO REALITY

Consider a claim to the following effect:

> "I not only take myself to be seeing a cat on the mat, but I maintain that this taking is justified in that I do actually do indeed see a cat on the mat."

Now when this is so, let us ask: What sort of substantiating evidence could I possibly have for this transit from appearance to reality? What is it that could reasonably be asked for here? Presumably it might be a manifold of considerations such as the following:

• Other people also claim to be seeing that cat on the mat
• Even animals appear to act likewise: for example, my cat-averse dog keeps well away from the mat
• Other experiences occur consonantly—for example when I prod the cat with a stick it miaus and hisses angrily

When this whole environing context of information and experience unfolds consonantly, one would clearly be entitled to stake the claim at issue. After all, what more will one possibly ask from than to have it that the whole of my own experience is supportively consonant and the course of other people's experience is—as best I can tell—duly conformable.

The crux of the matter is that once I have as much as one could reasonably ask for, then I am clearly warranted in staking an objective and veridical claims.

However, what is at issue here is not a factual thesis on the lines of:

• When those authorizing conditions hold, then the claim at issue is actually true but rather a practical principle of procedure on the lines of

- When those authorizing conditions hold, then the claim at issue is rationally warranted.

The justification of such a practical precept has two aspects:

1. This or nothing. If you are not prepared to allow other experiences to confirm an objective claim, then nothing ever will. This is the only possible route to objective information.
2. Experience teaches that if you proceed in this way then what you accept will generally (albeit not invariably) function successfully as objectively functional.

What we have here, then, is not a demonstrative proof of actual correctness, but a practical validation justified by considerations of functional efficacy. It is instructive here to contemplate the validation of reliance on expert advice. Its justification is not one of uncontestable correctness, but rather lies simply in the consideration that as best we can determine this is the best that one can do in the circumstances.

FURTHER LESSONS

When we accept a belief as true we have no sensible alternative but to hold that that is how reality actually stands. And so we arrive at the principle that: *True claims about things characterize reality as it really is* in the correlative manner or respect. And this principle represents an indissoluble link between epistemology and ontology.

To be sure, this coordination of reality with what is correctly thought still leaves open the question: which is the dependent and which is the independent variable in this thought/reality relationship. Does reality hinge on what is thought or does thought hinge on reality? Are we to be realists and hold that reality is as it is independently of what people think? Or are we to be idealists and hold that reality is as it is because thought presents it so.

What has to be said at this point is that a two-way street is at issue in that:

- What is *truly* thought to be so depends *functionally and existentially* on reality's being what it is. True thought is *ontologically* dependent upon reality.
- Our view of reality depends *conceptually* on what is truly thought to be so (because that is how the concept of truth functions). Whatever glimpse of reality we are able to achieve is *conceptually* dependent upon true thought.

The very conceptual linkage between being-warrantedly-thought-to-be and actually being is in principle a connection that works both ways.

An important lesson thus emerges from these deliberations:

- Reality does not stand apart from appearance but rather is coordinate with it when and wherever the appearances are correct. And—
- It is not just unproblematic but entirely appropriate to say that reality's being as is indispensable (conceptual) requisite for the truth of our claims about it.

But how is one to respond to deflationists who see truth as dispensable thanks to Alfred Tarski's thesis that "*p* is true" does no more than simply affirm *p*? To them we can say that such "deflationary" equivalence is also a two way street and that the equivalence at issue is just as much an inflationism that goes to show not the dispensability of claims to truth but their potential ubiquity in relation to fact and reality.

The position at issue might be characterized as *hermeneutic realism*. For it takes the stance that the features we ascribe to the world's realities on the basis of our cognitive interaction with them indeed are actually objective features of the real things at issue. However this should be seen as being so only insofar as our knowledge of them is indeed correct. So no idealism is at work here: our thought is true (when true it is) because reality is what it is, and not the other way around.

And so if life in the universe were extinguished, so that there is no thought whatsoever, most of reality would still remain substantially untouched. After all, the thought correlativity of reality does not hinge on what thought *does* do, but only on what it *could* do—or, to put it differently, what it *would* do if it were to accomplish its work properly. The linkage of reality to thought thus is not actualistic but potentialistic.

A concept audit of the ideas at issue with appearance and reality indicate that what is at issue with the reality/appearance distinction should not be seen as dealing with two distinct realms of being, as some philosophers would have it, but one single realm viewed from significantly different points of view, viz. that of authentic reality as it is, and that of authentic realty as it is (rightly or wrongly) thought to be. And the fact that we have no cognitive access to reality independently of what we think it to be does nothing to negate this circumstance.

#17

On Truth about Reality

ADEQUATION ISSUES

The traditional philosophical conception of truth takes it to be "adequation to reality" (*adaequatio ad rem*) by making claims that succeed in starting what is really and actually the case. Despite its seeming truism this construal of truth has significant ramifications and implications. To see this it helps to approach the matter in a somewhat round-about way.

Consider the mathematical equation

$$(A)\ \pi = 3.14159$$

As this stands we would have to say that this statement is not strictly and literally true. The value here claimed for π is only rough and approximate, seeing that many decimal places remain out of view. In accepting (A) we portray the actual situation in such a way that reality (the fully exact actual value of π) is mistakenly) identified with something (viz. 3.14159) that is no more than an approximation to it.

But now compare this situation with

$$(B)\ \text{John's weight} = 164\ \tfrac{1}{2}\ \text{pounds}$$

This statement is only seemingly analogous to (1). It is really something quite different. For here the pivotal item at issue (viz. John's weight) is not in fact a definitive and exact quantity. The idea that it is a precise number defined down to the level of micrograms—and even below—is absurd. There is no fixed exactness here. Variation is inevitable as one breathes in or out, swallows a grape, has a hair fall off one's head, and on and on. What is at issue is not a determinate quantity but something inherently imprecise, indefinite, and as it were blurry.

And so (B), unlike (A), is in fact true as it stands. What stands at the right of that = sign does full justice to what stands at the left. We are wholly entitled to say that 164 ½ pounds indeed is John's weight and not some rough approximation to it. For by its very nature as such, John's weight is not (actually) an exact quality—as is π, with its ever ongoing decimal points. That weight is—by its very nature—an *imprecise* quantity, and (B)'s specification of it is not approximate but exact. To say

(B*) John's Weight = 164.24867 pounds

would not be to present an improved and more accurate version of (B), but to make a claim that is somewhere between absurd and false.

ISSUES OF REALITY

But now consider the equation:

(C) The real state of affairs = the state of affairs as our best-achievable conceptual characterization purports it to be.

And now let us ask the $64 question:

(Q) Is the claim stated in (C) more closely analogous to (A) or to (B)? Is "our reality" an *approximation* to "reality itself" or is it (when adequate) simply a characterization of what is in fact so albeit in an indefinite and imprecise manner? Is (C) a claim that is not approximate but exact.

In effect the question here is whether appropriately deployed language merely approximates an (effectively uncharacterizable) reality, or whether (in ideal circumstances) it correctly portrays an imprecise and in some respects indefinite reality.

Kant—and many others with him—would here maintain the former option. For them (C) is analogous to (A). They see reality as something that is extra-linguistically ineffable and is at best open to an approximately, conceptually mediated characterization.

But, as the preceding concept audit indicates, another option is also open, namely that of seeing *C* on the analogy of (B).

On this (*B*)-analogous approach "our truth" is not a literally false approximation to an ineffable actuality, but rather presents the actual and authentic reality of things—at least in those instances when we get matters right. To put it somewhat figuratively, reality does not constitute a condition of things separate and different from appearance; it is, rather, a special situation of appearance itself—namely appearance in the special case of correctness or adequacy. When we are fortunate enough to set things right reality just exactly is what it appears to be and cognition does not *approximate* to reality but actually manages, in duly favorable circumstances to *characterize* it.

And so in the present case a concept audit neither substantiates nor invalidates that philosophically popular approximation thesis, but instead brings to light the prospect of a not implausible alternative to it.

Sameness and Change

SAMENESS THROUGH CHANGE

The widely quoted French aphorism has it that change is but more of the same *Plus* ça *change, plus c'est le même chose.* Yet is it true?

The Greek philosopher Heraclitus of Ephesus (ca. 540–480 B.C.) was famous even in his own day for the obscurity of his aphorisms. While only some dozens of his dicta survive, they have forever secured his reputation as the prophet of change, transiency, and the impermanence of things. Diogenes Laertius reports on his ideas as follows:

> Fire is the element, all things are exchange for fire and come into being by rarefaction and condensation; but of this he gives no clear explanation. All things come into being by conflict of opposites, and the sum of things flows like a stream. Further, all that is is limited and forms one world. And it is alternately born from fire and again resolved into fire in fixed cycles to all eternity, and this is determined by destiny. Of the opposites that which tends to birth or creation is called war and strife, and that which tends to destruction by fire is called concord and peace? Change he called a pathway up and down, and this determines the birth of the world.[1]

Although fire was the archetypical element in Heraclitus' theory of nature, water was his most famous analogy, and he will ever be known as the author of the celebrated epigram that "you cannot step into the same river twice":

Different waters ever flow upon those stepping into the same river . . . they scatter and combine . . . converge and diverge . . . approach and depart.[2]

In his story of the Ship of Theseus, the Greek historian and moralist Plutarch (ca. 48–125 A.D.) propounded a puzzle that soon spilt philosophers into rival schools:

The ship wherein *Theseus* and his young Athenians returned from Crete had thirty oars, and was preserved by the Athenians down even to the time of Demetrius Phalereus, for they took away the old planks as they decayed, putting in new and stronger timber in their place, in so much that this rebuilt ship became a standing example among the philosophers, for the logical question of the identity of things; one side holding that the ship remained the same, and the other contending that it was not the same.[3]

Much the same issue was posed much later by Thomas Hobbes' example of Sir John Cutler's stockings, which in the course of time wore out totally, bit by bit, with every hole repaired by darning needle and a thread until ultimately nothing of the original material recurred. Was the ultimate result still the same pair of stockings?

The large and diversified literature of science fiction raises a host of curious brain-manipulation issues along the lines of the following scenario:

> A perverse operative—mad scientist or wicked governmental agency—devises a brain-wave transfer apparatus that interchanges the <memories, tastes-likings-longings, or even total knowledge> of one individual with that of another.

Given this situation, the issue now arises which is which and who is who? The very concept of personal identity is thus brought into question. For example, does sameness of person depend on physical or on psychic continuity?

With this sort of issue in view, the contemporary literature of the philosophy of mind has witnessed an android invasion. Its landscape is full of robots whose communicative behavior is remarkably anthropoidal (are they "conscious" or not?) and of personality exchanges between people (which one is "the same person?"). In examining such issues, theorists purport to be clarifying matters, but their proceedings are actually of very dubious significance. For the assumptions at issue force apart what normally goes together—and do so in circumstances where the concepts we use are predicated upon a certain background of "normality."

CONTEXTUAL VARIATION

In the end, no supposedly clarificatory hypothesis should arbitrarily cut asunder what the basic facts of this world have joined together—at any rate not when trying to elucidate the concepts whose very being is predicated on those facts. For in the normal course of things those fact-coordinative concepts are only when the favorable cooperation of empirical circumstance avert difficulties that might otherwise stand in the way. But once we forgo reliance on these facts in the interests of theoretical neatness, the tension becomes destructive. For those attempted "clarifications" by the use of extreme cases and fanciful science-fiction examples engender pressures that burst the bonds that hold our concepts together. When we put reality aside and embark on far-fetched hypotheses, unmanageable difficulties crowd in upon us.

The tragic destiny of philosophy is to be constrained to pursue the interests of abstract rationality by means of concepts designed to accommodate the facts of experience; to have to probe the merely possible with the thought-instruments that have evolved to handle the concretely actual; to be constrained to address the necessary in the language of the contingent. In philosophy we have to be prepared for approximation and analogies that limit our generalizations to the normal and ordinary course of things. Hypotheses that cast our understanding of the world's ways to the winds thereby annihilate the very concepts in whose terms our deliberations must be conducted.[4]

Addressing such matters unavoidably involves basic issues of outlook and orientation. For if you function in the manner of an historian, there is no question but that you are bound to see the ship as the same; while for the issue of maritime insurance, it could well fail to count as such. So it is more than likely that when we disagree regarding "the *same X*"—the same person, or poem, or ship—what is actually at issue may well not be a single universal idea, but a variety of distinct matters differentiated by purposive considerations.

A concept audit of the idea of sameness, change, and the continuity of identity brings a significant fact to light, namely that there is no sameness to sameness. What being "the same X" involves actually hinges on the sort of thing that X happens to be: it all depends on the context of consideration. Where we speak of sameness in different contexts we use the same terminology but deal with different ideas. Exactly as with terms like "success" or "utility," the various cases at issue with such terminology differ in nature and are linked not by a shared uniformity of conceptual commonalties, but by a web of analogies among decidedly different situations. And so here, as elsewhere, concept auditing serves the useful function of preventing an unrewarding wild goose chase.

NOTES

1. Diogenes Laertius, *Lives of Eminent Philosopher*, IX, sect's 6–7. (Tr. R. D. Hicks).

2. Kirk, Raven, Schofield, *The Pre-Socratic Philosophers* (Cambridge: Cambridge University Press, 1957), p, 195.

3. Plutarch, *Life of Theseus*.

4. Further readings on these topics include Roderick M. Chisholm, *Person and Object* (La Salle: Open Court, 1976); Fred d. Miller, Jr., and Nicholas D. Smith, *Thought Probes* (Englewood Cliffs: Prentice Hall, 1980); Nicholas Rescher, *Philosophical Standardism* (Pittsburgh: University of Pittsburgh Press, 1994); Sydney Shoemaker and Richard Swinburne, *Personal Identity* (Oxford: Blackwell, 1984).

#19

Origination Issues

The Law of Causality stipulates that all occurrences must have causal explanations. And the wide ranging acceptance of this principle appears to create difficulties for beginnings and initiations, which seemingly require an earlier occurrence to constitute the course of the developments at issue. But such a line of thought is predicated in insufficient heed of the conceptual lay of the land. For there is in fact no need to regard a beginning or initiation as itself constituting an occurrence within the range at issue.

Thus, let it be that the time period during which the development at issue obtains has the form of what the mathematicians would characterize as an open interval, as per Figure 19.1

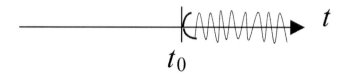

$$t_0 \qquad t$$

Figure 19.1

Then at any time up to *and including* t_0 the development in questions does *not* obtain, while at any time after (but not including) t_0 it does obtain. In consequence, at any time of its obtaining there is an earlier time when it also obtains yet doing so without any regression beyond t_0. And so its condition at the later time can in principle be causally accounted for in terms of its earlier condition. There is in principle perfect conformity with the Law of Causality—the origination of the development itself notwithstanding.

Here, even though there is no "moment of creation" when the development at issue first obtains nevertheless this development originates in time: up to (and including) a certain point it does not exist, and thereafter it does.

And of course the same story can be told in reverse. For if the timespan of the existence of a development is also an open instance as per Figure 19.2

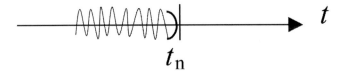

t_n

Figure 19.2

Then there is no last time of its realization, or no "moment of death" to its life story. At any and every time up to an entry point it exists, but once that point is reached it no longer does so. Its existence is without a last moment. At any and every point of its lifespan it yet has a future. And yet immoral it is not.

Accordingly, careful heed of the conceptual situate shows that the Law of Causality can operate with seamless efficacy while nevertheless dispensing with any need to account for initiation events—simply and solely because such events do not belong to the manifold of occurrence at all. Like *starting* to fall (instead of falling) or *winning* a race (instead of running in it) such beginnings and completions are not constituent *parts* of the series of occurrences but descriptive *aspects* of its format. And so, a concept audit of the relevant idea goes to show that the Law of Causality can prevail even without addressing such evaluations.

#20

Shaping Ideas

SELF-EXEMPLIFICATION IN PLATO'S THEORY OF IDEAS

Idealistic philosophers since Plato have inclined to ascribing to ideas themselves the very features at issue in their signification. As these theorists saw it, there was something simple about simplicity and something complex about complexity. The very idea of nastiness had to be somewhat nasty; the idea of a horse had to have manifest an equine aspect. Ideas or conceptions were seen as being by nature self-reflective and, as it were, autodescriptive.

The medieval schoolmen—or at any rate the more rigorous logicians among them—viewed this doctrine of ideational self-exemplification as far-fetched. Drawn to the doctrine of nominalism, they saw ideas as correlated to and encapsulated within terminology—within words or word families. The idea of cats, for example was encompassed in such words as feline, pussy, lion, and the like. Ideas accordingly live embodied in words, and this was seen to stand in the way of being self-illustrative. Which of these conflicting views is one to endorse?

DIRECT VERSUS INDIRECT DISCOURSE

The logic of the matter shows that with words and word complexes such as sentences we must distinguish between the nature of the thing expressed and the nature of its expression. Consider, for instance, such statements as:

The term *German* means German, but yet is not German but English.
The word *long* is not long but short.
As an idea, *incomprehensible* means unintelligible, but it is certainly not so.

As such examples show, the sorts of features possessed by our terminological means of discourse stand quite apart from those of the substantive contentions that are at issue.

To mark this insight clearly we do well to join the medieval schoolmen in doing what they did best: drawing a distinction.

Consider, they in effect said, such claims as "New is new" or "Short is short." In these sentences those repeated words look to be the same. But appearances are very deceptive here since in fact very different things are at issue. Thus considered these claims come to

- The ideas of what is *new* is new

    and

- The word *short* is short

Here, the italicized word is not used directly in its standard way (in what the medievals called direct discourse: *oratio directa*) as is the case with its initial occurrence. It is instead used obliquely to represent not the standard meaning, but rather the word is expressive that used to convey it. And they called this procedure *oratio obliqua*, oblique discourse.

And as they saw is, the same situation comes to the fore in such contrasts as that between

- Henry said "the cat is on the mat"

    and

- Henry said that the cat is on the mat

The second statement here relates to the substance (or message) at issue in what Henry said: the first to the words used to convey that message. Distinctly different things are at issue here—as becomes very clear when we add the word "silently" at the end.

THE LESSON

While the medieval terminology of *direct/indirect discourse* was then new, its point with respect to the difference between *using* words and *talking about* them is perfectly plain and commonsensical, and was no doubt envisioned right along. And once this distinction is recognized as the fruit of an appropriate concept audit, any temptation to ascribe to ideas themselves, the features at issue with their mode of identification is bound to vanish. No problems will arise from acknowledging that there is nothing simple about the idea of simplicity and nothing sweet about the idea of sweetness. The mode or manner of reference or ideation is often detached from what is being considered. The Platonic theory of ideational self-instantiation now becomes gravely undermined.

#21

Construing Necessitation

QUALIFIER PLACEMENT PROBLEMS

How is one to understand the frequent claims of philosophers to the effect that something is necessary because something else is the case—as with Descartes *cogito ergo sum.*

The fact is that two very different sorts of contentions are at issue with respect to such matters of conditional necessity, namely

$$\text{necessarily: if } A \text{ then } B \text{ (symbolically: } \Box(A \to B)\text{)}$$

and

$$\text{if } A, \text{ then necessarily } B \text{ (symbolically: } A \to \Box B\text{)}$$

In the former case necessity pertains to the implication relation as a whole, while in the second case it pertains to the consequent alone. (The medieval logicians accordingly distinguished between consequential and consequent necessity *necessitas consequentiae* and *necessitas consequentis.*)

It is instructive to compare this situation with the analogous case of negation in place of necessity:

(1) By no means: If A, then B—or symbolically: $\sim(A \to B)$

and

(2) If A, then by no means B—or symbolically: $(A \to \sim B)$

It is clear that consequential and consequent negation involves obviously different claims. This becomes evident when

$$A = \text{You are in France}$$

$$B = \text{You are in Paris}$$

Here the (1)-style thesis is of course true: It is certainly not the case that: If you are in France then you are in Paris. But the (2)-style thesis is "If you are in France then you are not in Paris," which is clearly false. That qualifier placement makes a decisive difference. And this is clearly also going to be so with necessitation.

Accordingly, a correct audit of the relevant ideas shows that there is a dramatic difference between two construals of implicational necessity.

IMPLICATIONS

The point at issue in this concept audit is especially critical for clarity in discussing matters of causal determination and free will. For it is one thing to say

1. In view of the harmony between brain states and thought states, when your brain is in state S, then your mind is in the corresponding state S'.
2. In view of harmony between brain states and thought states, when your brain is in state S, then your mind is necessary in the corresponding state S'.

If (as seems plausible) there is a harmonious correlation between brain states and mind states, then (1) may well be true. But this fact (if fact it is) neither validates the very different thesis (2), nor yet does it do anything whatsoever to impede the prospect of free will. For it is clear that the coordination of mind and brain is a two-way street along which determinative influence can travel in either direction. As with a child's teeter-totter rigid coordination does not determine who is in charge.

Conceptual Horizons

COGNITIVE LIMITS

We humans cannot step outside thought space any more than we can step outside physical space. No doubt we can move in the realm of thought from one place to another that is very different from it. But at any given stage of cognitive endeavor people are placed within a particular, context-characteristic conceptual environment. And our position in thought space—just like our position in actual space—has its horizons, which in the present case are conceptual rather than visual.

The limits of our culture set the conceptual limitations of our thought. Cicero might well have asked—as did Harry Truman on encountering Pittsburgh politics—"What the hell is a Prothonotary?" Aristotle was an exceedingly clever thinker. But one could never have *explained* quantum theory to him within the concept scheme of this own familiar Greek. One would have to *teach* it to him, in the way on which present-day students are taught. The fact it is that the lexicographic range of our ideas and concepts—however large—sets corresponding limits to our cognate by limiting our conceptual reach.

However, while we know *that* there are ideas we cannot express, we (by hypothesis) do not—and indeed cannot—know *what* they are. We know *that* there are facts we do not know, but (by hypothesis) cannot identify them. We have the capacity to learn and to discover to expound our conceptual horizons. But with any mode of innovation we can never say in advance just where it will lead us.

The temporal aspect of knowledge comes to the fore at this point. One need not be a very profound metaphysician to realize that the things of this universe exist in time. And our imperfect access to cognition about the future is a fertile source of unknowable facts and intractable questions. Consider, for instance:

- What is an example of a truth that will not be discovered until next year?
- What is a fact that no one will realize until the next century?

And here too generalization is possible:

- What is an example of a truth that no one will ever state?
- What is an instance of an idea that will never occur to anyone?

In all such cases, we are once again in the realm of cognitive bafflement engendered by intractable questions. And one cannot evade this by claiming that the reasons for one's incapacity is, that such questions just are not answerable at all—that they inherently have no answers and that there is no fact of the matter here. There indeed are facts of the matter. It is just that we cannot get a cognitive grip on them.

The crux here is that in cognitive matters, at least, the present cannot speak for the future. There are questions no one can answer before their time. Prediction is thus a fertile source of unanswerable questions. Take just one example:

- For as long as intelligent life continues to exist somebody will always pose a question that will go unresolved for at least 1000 years.

Here we have a clear instance of an undecidable factual proposition. For a decisive resolution becomes impracticable in such cases where generality mixes with particularity so that both assertion and denial involves an unsurveyable universality.

NONINSTANTIABLE PROPERTIES AND VAGRANT PREDICATES

The cognitive intractability of certain temporalized issues has wider implications.

On this basis we can also contemplate the prospect of globally intractable questions—questions which, despite having correct answers, are nevertheless such that nobody (among finite intelligences at least) can possibly be in a position to answer them (in the strict sense described at the outset). Thus consider such questions as:

- What is an example of a problem that will never be considered by any human being?

• What is an example of an idea that will never occur to any human being?

And there are many instances of this phenomena seeing that no one can meet the challenge of providing examples of such things as

• being an idea that has never occurred to anybody?
• being an occurrence is there that no one ever mentions?
• being a person who has passed into total oblivion.
• being an idea no one any longer mentions.

While there undoubtedly are such items, they of course cannot possibly be instantiated so that the correlative example-demanding questions constitute inherently unanswerable insolubilia.

In all such cases, the particular items that would render a contention of the format $(\exists u)Fu$ true are *referentially inaccessible*: to indicate any of them individually and specifically as instantiations of the predicate at issue is *ipso facto* to unravel them as so-characterized items. And so, noninstantiability itself is certainly not something that is noninstantiable: many instances are available along the lines of:

—being an ever-unstated fact (contention, truth, theory, etc.).
—being a never-mentioned topic (idea, object, etc.).
—being someone whom everyone has forgotten.
—being an issue no one has thought about since the sixteenth century.

In the light of these considerations, the positivist dogma that a question can qualify as empirically meaningful only if it is in principle possible for a finite knower to answer it (correctly) becomes problematic. Cognitive positivism is not a plausible prospect.

The conception of an applicable but nevertheless noninstantiable predicate comes to the fore at this point. Such predicates are *"vagrant"* in the sense of *having no known address or fixed abode*. Though they indeed have applications, these cannot be specifically instanced—they cannot be pinned down and located in a particular spot. Accordingly we have it that:

F is a *vagrant* predicate iff $(\exists u)Fu$ is true while nevertheless Fu_0 is false for each and every specifically identified u_0.

For the sake of contrast, consider such further uninstantiable predicates as

—being a book no one has ever read.
—being a sunset never witnessed by any member of *Homo sapiens*.

Such items may be difficult to instantiate—but certainly not impossible. The former could be instantiated by author and title; the latter by place and date. In neither case will an instantiation unravel that item as described. Being read is not indispensably essential to books, nor being seen to sunsets: being an unread book or being an unwitnessed sunset involves no contradiction in terms. By contrast, however, with actual vagrancy epistemic inaccessibility is built into the specification at issue. Here we have predicates of such a sort that one can show on the basis of general principles that there must be items to which they apply, while nevertheless one can also establish that no such items can ever be concretely identified.[1] In such cases we are dealing with something that unquestionably exists, but by its very nature precludes of identification by way of specification or illustration.

The existence of vagrant predicates shows that applicability and instantiability do not amount to the same thing. By definition, vagrant predicates will be applicable: there indeed are items to which they apply. However, this circumstance will always have to be something that must be claimed on the basis of general principles, doing so by means of concretely identified instances is, by hypothesis, infeasible.

LESSONS

A concept audit of terminology in the range of knowledge-truth-understanding has significant implications for philosophical deliberations relating to skepticism. One of these is that the prospect of completed knowledge is unrealizable. Neither radically nor collectively can we finite beings possibly obtain cognitive access to the totality of truth.

On the other hand, a radical skepticism or the sort that maintains "we really know nothing whatsoever—the securing of knowledge is beyond our powers"—must be ruled out. There are facts whose realization we cannot avoid once we set out to deliberate about such matters. The realization that our knowledge is incomplete—that there are facts we do not know—is prominent among these. The radical skeptic whose skepticism denies him the prospect of getting to know that this is so is thereby sawing off the limb in which his own position is suspended. A concept audit of the relevant ideas series to show that just as our knowledge has its inherent limits so this is also the case with our skepticism about it.

NOTE

1. Reference, to be sure, does not require identification. A uniquely characterizing description on the order of "the tallest person in the room" will single out a particular individual without specifically identifying him.

#23

Language Limits

FACTS ARE TRANSDENUMERABLE

A key consideration for the much controverted issue of the limitations of human knowledge lies in the circumstance that our knowledge of fact is linguistically mediated while the domain of fact itself transcends the limits of language.

Statements in general—and therefore true statements in particular—can be enumerated, and truths are consequently denumerable in number. But there is good reason to suppose that this will not hold for facts. On the contrary, there is every reason to think that, reality being what it is, there will be an uncountably large manifold of facts.

The reality of it is that facts, unlike truths, cannot be enumerated: *no listing of fact-presenting truths—not even one of infinite length—can possibly manage to constitute a complete register of facts.* Any attempt to register-fact-as-a-whole will founder: the list is bound to be incomplete because there are facts about the list-as-a-whole which no single entry can encompass.

We thus arrive at one of the key theses of these deliberations:

Thesis 1: *The Transdenumerability of Facts.* The manifold of fact is transdenumerably infinite.

The idea of a complete listing of all the facts is manifestly impracticable. For consider the following statement. *"The list F of stated facts fails to have this statement on it."* But now suppose this statement to be on the list. Then it clearly does not state a fact, so that the list is after all not a list of the facts (contrary to hypothesis). And so it must be left off the list. But then in consequence that list will not be complete since the statement is true. Facts, that is to say, can never be listed *in toto* because there will always be further facts—facts about the entire list itself—that a supposedly complete list could not manage to register.

This conclusion can be rendered more graphic by the following considerations. Suppose that the list F

$$F: f_1, f_2, f_3, \ldots$$

were to constitute a *complete* enumeration of all facts. And now consider the statement

(Z) the list F takes the form $f_1, f_2, f_3, \ldots$

By hypothesis, this statement will present a fact. So if F is indeed a complete listing of *all* facts, then there will be an integer k such that

$$Z = f_k$$

Accordingly, Z itself will occupy the kth place on the F listing, so that

$$f_k = \text{the list } L \text{ takes the form } f_1, f_2, f_3, \ldots f_k, \ldots$$

But this would require f_k to be an expanded version of itself, which is absurd. With the kth position of the F listing *already* occupied by f_k we cannot also squeeze that complex f_k-involving thesis into it.

The crux here is simply that any supposedly complete listing of facts

$$f_1, f_2, f_3 \ldots$$

will itself exhibit, as a whole, certain features that none of its individual members can encompass. Once those individual entries are fixed and the series is defined, there will be further facts about that series-as-a-whole that its members themselves cannot articulate.

Moreover, the point at issue can also be made via an analogue of the diagonal argument that is standardly used to show that no list of real numbers can manage to include all of them, thereby establishing the transdenumerability of the reals. Thus imagine a supposedly complete inventory of *independent* facts, using logic to streamline the purported fact inventory into a condition of greater informative tidiness through the elimination of inferential redundancies, so that every remaining item adds some information to what has gone before. The argument for the transdenumerability of fact can now be developed as follows.

Let it be that (for the sake of *reductio ad absurdum* argumentation) that the inventory

$$f_1, f_2, f_3, \ldots$$

represents our (nonredundant but yet purportedly *complete*) listing of facts. Then by the supposition of *factuality* we have $(\forall i)f_i$. And further by the supposition of *completeness* we have it that

$$(\forall p)(p \to (\exists i)[f_i \to p])$$

Moreover, by the aforementioned supposition of *nonredundancy*, each member of the sequence adds something quite new to what has gone before.

$$(\forall i)(\forall j)[i < j \to \sim[(f_1 \& f_2 \& \ldots \& f_i) \to f_j)]$$

Consider now the following course of reasoning.

(1) $(\forall i)f_i$ by "factuality"
(2) $(\forall j)f_j \to (\exists i)(f_i \to (\forall j)f_j)$ from (1) by
     $(\forall j)f_j$ for p
     via the substitution of
(3) $(\exists i)(f_i \to (\forall j)f_j)$ from (1), (2), by "completeness"

But (3) contradicts nonredundancy. This *reductio ad absurdum* of our hypothesis indicates that facts are necessarily be too numerous for complete enumeration.

So here quantity matters and we arrive at

Thesis 2. *There are quantitatively more facts than truths* seeing that the facts are too numerous for enumerabilty.

The salient point is that occurrent knowledge, being language-encorporated, can in principle be inventories by aggregate compilation in one vastly long list. And even potential knowledge, which admits of (a doubtless vastly complex) axiomatization will run to no more than a denumerably infinite listing. But there is no basis for (and indeed very good reason against) seeing the realm of *actual fact* as admitting of presentation by a listing—be it finite or infinite. The overall manifold of fact simply cannot be inventory (if only because any such inventory—even if achievable, per impossible—would itself engender infinitude of further facts).

Reality, so we must suppose, is inexhaustibly complex. Its *detail* (as Leibniz wanted to call it) is bottomless. Thus while statements in general, and therefore true statements in particular, can be enumerated, so that truths are denumerable in number—there is no reason to suppose that the same will hold for facts. On the contrary, there is every reason to think that, reality being what it is, there will be an uncountably vast manifold of facts.

THE SHORTFALL OF LANGUAGE

However the numerical diversity at issue does not go far enough. For it only shows that there are facts that never will be stated: it does not show that there are facts that *cannot* be stated. (Think here again of the situation of the Musical Chairs game.)

The realm of fact is endlessly complex, detailed, and diversified in its make-up. It is not only possible but (apparently) likely that we live in a world that is not digital but analogue and whose manifold of states of affairs is simply too rich to be fully comprehended by our linguistically digital means. To all visible appearances the domain of fact transcends the limits of our capacity to *express* it, and *a fortiori* those of our capacity to canvass it.

In confronting any landscape in nature, our representation of it in propositional discourse or thought—our description-scape, so to speak—is invariably far less complex and inevitably suppresses a vast amount of detail. (Even the physics of discrete quanta requires continuous—and thus nondiscrete— parameters for its characterization.)

Descriptive truth is to actual fact what a motion-picture film is to reality— a merely discretized approximation. Cognition, being bound to language, is digital and sequentially linear. Reality, by contrast, is analogue and replete with feedback loops and nonsequentially systemic interrelations. It should thus not be seen as all that surprising that the two cannot be brought into smooth alignment. The comparative limitedness of language-encapsulable truth points to an inevitable limitedness of knowledge.

We here come to what is, in effect, the metaphysical insight that that range of fact about anything real is effectively inexhaustible. There is, in principle, no end to what can be said regarding any natural object whatsoever, seeing that as best we can tell, there is no limit to the world's ever-increasing complexity that comes to view with our ever-increasing technologically mediated grasp of its detail. And this means that any attempt to register-fact-as-a-whole will founder: the list is bound to be incomplete because there are facts about the list-as-a-whole which no single entry can encompass. (There will always be a fact about any set of facts that is not a member of that set itself.)

The reality of it is that the domain of fact is ampler than that of truth so that language cannot capture the entirety of fact. We live in a world that is not digital but analogue and so the manifold of states of affairs is simply too rich to be fully comprehended by our linguistically digital means.[1] The domain of fact inevitably transcends the limits of our capacity to *express* it, and *a fortiori* those of our capacity to canvass it in overt detail. Truth is to fact what moving pictures are to reality—a merely discretized approximation.

COGNITIVE POVERTY

There can be no doubt that ignorance exacts its price in incomprehension. And here it helps to consider the matter in a somewhat theological light. The world we live in is a manifold that is not of our making but of Reality's—of Gods if you will.

What is at issue might be called Isaiah's Law on the basis of the verse: "For as the heavens are higher than the earth, so are my ways higher than your ways, and my thoughts than your thoughts."[2]

Fundamental law of epistemology is at work here, to wit, that *a mind of lesser power is for this very reason unable to understand adequately the workings of a mind of greater power*. To be sure, the weaker mind can doubtless realize *that* the stronger can solve problems it itself cannot. But it cannot understand *how* it is able to do so. An intellect that can only just manage to do well at tic-tac-toe cannot possibly comprehend the ways of one that is expert at chess.

Consider in this light the vast disparity of computational power between a mathematical tyro like most of us and a mathematical prodigy like Ramanujan. Not only cannot our tyro manage to answer the number-theoretic question that such a genius resolves in the blink of an eye, but the tyro cannot even begin to understand the processes and procedures that the Indian genius employs. As far as the tyro is concerned, it is all sheer wizardry. No doubt once an answer is given he can check its correctness. But actually finding the answer is something which that lesser intellect cannot manage—the how of the business lies beyond its grasp. And, for much the same sort of reason, a mind of lesser power cannot discover what the question-resolving limits of a mind of greater power are. It can never say with warranted assurance where the limits of question-resolving power lie. (In some instances it may be able to say what's in and what's out, but never map the dividing boundary.)

It is not simply that a more powerful mind will know more facts than a less powerful one, but that its conceptual machinery is ampler in encompassing ideas and issues that lie altogether outside the conceptual horizon of its less powerful compeers.

Now insofar as the relation of a lesser toward a higher intelligence is substantially analogous to the relation between an earlier state of science and a later state, some instructive lessons emerge. It is not that Aristotle could not have comprehended quantum theory—he was a very smart fellow and could certainly have learned. But what he could not have done is to formulate quantum theory within his own conceptual framework, his own familiar terms of reference. The very ideas at issue lay outside of the conceptual horizon of Aristotle's science, and like present-day students he would have had to master them from the ground up. Just this sort of thing is at issue with the relation of a less powerful intelligence to a more powerful one. It has been said insightfully that from the vantage point of a less developed technology another, substantially advanced technology is indistinguishable from magic. And exactly the same holds for a more advanced *conceptual* (rather than physical) technology.

It is instructive to contemplate in this light the hopeless difficulties encountered nowadays in the popularization of physics—of trying to characterize the implications of quantum theory and relativity theory for cosmology into the subscientific language of everyday life. A classic *obiter dictum* of Niels Bohr is relevant: "We must be clear that, when it comes to atoms, language can be used only as in poetry." Alas, we have to recognize that in philosophy, too, we are in the final analysis, something of the same position. In the history of culture, *Homo sapiens* began their quest for knowledge in the realm of poetry. And in the end it seems that we are destined to remain at this starting point in some respects.

All the same, notwithstanding our cognitive limitedness as finite beings, there are nevertheless no boundaries—no *determinate* limits—to the manifold of discoverable fact. And here Kant was right—even on the Leibnizian principles considered earlier in the present discussion. For while the cognitive range of finite beings is indeed limited, it is also boundless because it is not restricted in a way that blocks the prospect of cognitive access to ever new and ongoingly more informative facts providing an ever ampler and ever more adequate account of reality.

The logocentric philosophers who think that language analysis can do it all for us need to have another think about it.

NOTES

1. Wittgenstein writes "logic is not a body of doctrine, but a mirror-image of the world" (*Tractatus*, 6.13). This surely gets it wrong: logic is one instrumentality (among others) for organizing our thought about the world, and this thought is (as best and at most) a venture in *describing* or *conceiving* the world and its modus operandi in

a way that—life being what it is—will inevitably be imperfect, and incomplete. And so any talk of mirroring is a totally unrealistic exaggeration here.

   2. *Isaiah*, 58:9.

#24

On Certainty

MODES OF CERTAINTY

Philosophers since Descartes have insisted that knowledge must be certain. But they have not been so ready to acknowledge—as ordinary folks would readily do—that there are two decidedly different types of certainty:

- something is *absolutely* certain if it is certain beyond any *possible* doubt.
- something is *effectively* certain if it is certain beyond any *reasonable* doubt.

The former is a matter of *absolute* or *categorical or transcendental* certainty, the latter one of *virtual* or *practical or mundane* certainty.

Now when we say that knowledge must be certain, it is clearly the second that we do (or should!) have in view. After all, knowledge is a concept that does work for us in everyday-life communication. The certainty of knowledge is the certain of life—the sort of certainly at issue with contentions on the order of "Houses can be built of brick," "All men have bodies," and the like—the sorts of claims that are the staple of the world we live in.

Consider the example of a dialectical situation of a knowledge-claim subject to sequential challenges:

A: This is a pen.

B: Are you quite certain?

A: Of course.

B: Do you actually know it?

A: Yes, quite so.

B: But how can you be sure it's not something done with mirrors?

A: I brought it in myself two hours ago and it's in my pocket, and I've used it. So I think the mirror possibility can safely be eliminated.

B: But are you sure no trickster has put a clever pen-substitute in its place?

A: No one has been here until you came, and I've been writing with it.

B: But what if a wicked Cartesian demon has been deceiving you in all this?

A: ?!?!?!

It is clear that when the challenger has been pushed to his final move here he has "overstepped the bounds" of reasonable doubt, and has left the sphere of plausible challenges based upon real prospects of error, pursuing the will-of-the-wisps of purely theoretical and altogether hyperbolic worriments. (We need not be in a position positively to rule out uncannily real dreams, deceitful demons, powerful evil scientists operating remotely from other galaxies, etc.) And one can easily construct other such dialogical exercises, all yielding the same lesson: that in such interrogative situations, the series of challenges is soon forced to a recourse to absurdity. One reaches the level of obstacles it is in principle impossible to remove and whose removal cannot for that very reason reasonably be demanded.

There are, moreover, two further modes of certainty, the personal ("I am certain") and the impersonal ("It is certain"). And there is an inherent conceptual connection between them. For when I am certain of something, and am further convinced that there is nothing that stands in its way apart from totally unrealistic obstacles (evil Cartesian deceivers, malignant hypnotists, life-is-but-a-dream supposition, or the like), then rational conjecture—and everyday-life understandings as well—will entitle me to make the (conscientiously defeasible) move from personal to impersonal certainty.

IMPLICATIONS FOR KNOWLEDGE

The key point is that the terminology of our everyday discourse—claims to knowledge and to certainty included—is governed by common-sense principles and conventions of ordinary usage. For our epistemological procedures—explanation, substantiation, justification, and the rest—are all essentially social acts performed in the context of a communal interchange of ideas and information that is subject to communally established ground rules. A fundamental communicative purpose underlies all these probative activities. The end of the road of the process of justification is obviously reached when anything further that could be brought in would be less plausible than what is already at hand. Even as one must not explain an obscurity by something yet more obscure (*non est explicanda obscurum per obscurior*), so we must not defend the doubtful by what is yet more dubious. In the preceding dialogue, a stage is reached when the existence of the pen in question is (*ex hypothesi*) something that is as sure under the epistemic circumstances at issue as one could ever be of supporting further considerations that could be adduced on its behalf. And when this stage is reached, there is no point in going on.[1]

To say that a claim is effectively certain is to say that it is *as certain as something of its kind could possibly be*. To be sure, certainty is not a matter of degree—one certain thing is not more or less certain than another. But this uncontested fact of noncomparability does not mean that there cannot be different contexts for certainty—that the certainties of Assyriology cannot differ in character from those of biochemistry.

The "certainty" of knowledge claims can seemingly be understood in two very different perspectives:

1. As an unattainable ideal, a condition at which a knowledge claim aims but which in the very nature of things it cannot attain—to its own decisive detriment.
2. As an assurance, a promise, a guarantee that everything needful has been done for the ascertainment of the knowledge claim, and this must be construed in socially oriented terms as a real-life resource of the operative dynamics of communication.

Various philosophers—and most skeptics—insist on the former construal, an insistence which is as unnecessary as it is unrealistic. For it is surely the second, mundane or realistic interpretation that is operative in the conception of knowledge we actually use in our actual everyday-life proceedings.

And so, once held the lessons of a proper concept-audit of the relevant terms—certainty, knowledge, credibility, substantiation—then skepticism's thesis that nothing is ever sufficiently certain to deserve being characterized as knowledge falls by the wayside.

NOTE

1. "What I mean is this: that my not having been on the moon is as sure a thing for me as any grounds I could (possibly) give for it." (Ludwig Wittgenstein, *On Certainty* [Oxford: Basil Blackwell, 1961]. Sect. III; cf. also Sect. 516.)

#25

Timeless Truth?

Philosophy, so Spinoza tells us, is supposed to deal with things "from the perspective of eternity" (*sub specie aeternitatis*). He held that its mission is to deal with eternal verities and timeless truths. Easier said than done.

To begin with, just what is a timeless truth? Is it a truth that is atemporal—dealing with matters altogether out of range of temporal considerations, like "1 + 1 = 2" and other mathematical facts? Is it a truth that deals with facts that are true at every point in time, such as "There are events taking place now that have never occurred before." And note that if something is true at some time then there are corresponding facts that are true at every time. Thus if "It is raining now in London" is true at Noon on January 1, 2000, then "There is rain in London on January 1, 2000" is a truth that holds always and everywhere.

It will obviously not do to say that truths are timeless if they are such that people should always acknowledge and never dissent from them. For this of course true of all truths whatsoever. (No one should ever deny that Napoleon was born in Corsica.)

Again it will not do to truths that are timeless unless some people in every age where people exists recognize and acknowledge them. For this is certainly false—for sure with respect to prehistoric man and very possibly in certain "dark ages."

It is evident that some statements are temporally variable. Like "It is raining go Toronto" or "John shook hands with Bob yesterday" they are true at some time and not others. But philosophy—like natural science—has no concern with those variably true statements. Yet nevertheless to charge philosophy with having to deal with timeless truths is to obfuscate matters by par at the very outset with a problematic issue whose substance is murky and whose complications are vast.

On the other hand, matters would be much simplified if one spoke of time-less *questions* or *problems* or *issues* instead of truths. There of course would be questions (etc.) that arise in every age and engage the interests of people in every successive era—matters that never cease to be relevant to the human condition and interesting to many of its exemplars.

And this circumstance not only illustrates the interesting point that in phi-losophy it is easier to provide questions than answers but indicates the further need to be clear and precise about exactly what those questions are. For of course the answer is bound to depend on just exactly what the questions are.

#26

Assessing Acceptability

NONACCEPTANCE VERSUS REJECTION

A report is *rejected* when one endorses its denial; it is *declined* when one suspends judgment regarding its affirmation. This important distinction is often insufficiently heeded in the epistemology of information processing. For in line with its distinction there are two reactions to the reliability of sources. They can be deemed untrustworthy in the sense that one systemically declines to accept their claims and suspends judgment about them. Or they can be deemed deceptive in that one inclines to reject their reports and accept the contrary of what they claim. In the former case we treat our sources with unbelief, in the latter with disbelief. When we have lost confidence in the competence of a source, we refrain from accepting its reports. When we actually distrust the source—when we think it has become corrupted or even "turned"—then we will outright disbelieve its claims. (Note that the second situation is actually more informative: it obliquely provides us with information in hand, whereas the former leaves a blank. Its being reported by a deceptive source affects our judgment of the *probability* of the truth of what is reported, by way of decreasing it.)

When are we going to accept a claim to supposed fact and add it to the stock of our beliefs—our putative knowledge? This is obviously an issue that engages both the philosophers and the ordinary man. Philosophers incline to rely on Bishop Butler's idea that probability is the guide of life. Probability, in the sense of harmonization with the body of already available knowledge is seen as the pivot. Accordingly, these theorists base their proceeding on the substantiating evidence that speaks for the substantive content of a claim.

However, in actual practice we frequently have recourse to another line of consideration, namely source reliability. In many cases we ourselves simply do not possess enough information or sufficient expertise to make an informed judgment on such matters and are largely or wholly dependent on the reliability of a reporting informant. In these circumstances our acceptance of a report will depend not on our evaluation of its substance, but rather on our evaluation of its source—not on the statement but on the stater. If the source is deemed reliable we will accept what it claims, if not, then not.

To be sure, problems will arise in this context if the report at issue emanates from a source we deem to be highly reliable but is substantively doubtful on the basis of the information we otherwise have on the topic. When source reliability conflicts with report improbability we are invariably perplexed. When the reverse is the case there is, of course, no problem: We simply ignore the report.

PROBABILITY ISSUES

Let it be that we adjudge both the *competence of a source*, and the *inherent probability of its claims* on a tripartite scale of high/middling/low. Then we obtain a manifold categorization of the claims at issue as per the tabulation of Figure 26.1.

The problem situation here is that of the questioned diagonal. There is no hard-and-fast rules for acceptability in such situations. The resolution can go one way or the other depending on the circumstances of the particular case.

Overall, a concept audit of the terms relating to report acceptability provides a pathway to understanding pivotal aspects of the matter. For important to realize that with respect to reports acceptability and probability are two different and substantially independent issues. In some circumstances of reportage an inherently improbable claim may deserve acceptance, and, counterwise, a very probable one may need to be rejected. The probative situation in matters of reportage presents a complex challenge whose sensible resolution requires close attention to matters of informative detail.

Display 1
ASSESSMENT OF CLAIM ACCEPTABILITY

Assumed Competence
of the Source

		H	M	L
	H	A	A	?
Inherent				
Probability	M	A	?	S
of the Claim				
	L	?	S	S

Note: Here we have:

A = Accept
S = Suspend
? = Problematic (Accept or suspend according to circumstances)

COMMENT: As regards that shaded entry it should be stressed that the idea that highly probable claims should routinely be accepted is unraveled by the well-known Lottery Paradox. At most they should be seen as provisionally acceptable.

Figure 26.1

#27

Value Neutrality in Science

IS/OUGHT SEPARATION AND VALUE EXCLUSION FROM SCIENCE

The thesis that the sciences—and the social sciences in particular—should be value-free has figured prominently in philosophy since the early twentieth century, particularly under the influence of the German sociologist Max Weber (1864–1920).[1] The basic idea is that scientific claims should be formulated and validated impersonally, without involving the potentially variable value orientations of different individuals. Science should deal in observable facts, with issues of value—of deservability, preferability, normativity, objection, and the like—left to individuals to resolve independently on their own. Even as physicists look to observably stable phenomenon ("repeatability of experiments"), so the social sciences shall look to phenomena that are universally accessible, independently of potentially idiosyncratic orientations of particular individuals or groups. To be sure, the social sciences will investigate—at arm's length—the way in which people commit themselves to values, but any and all endorsement or espousal of those values themselves is to be proscribed.

The fact/value distinction is generally drawn on essentially terminological grounds. The idea is that fact statements simply maintain what is available to observation and inference therefrom. They report on reality's descriptive make-up. Value statements by contrast, are not factual but axiological. They have a normative and axiological dimension, owing to an involvement of some evaluative terms that give expression to placement along a positive/negative, favorable/unfavorable divide. So that cats chase mice is a factual claim. That it is a good (or bad) thing that cats chase mice is evaluative. The

115

former may be germane to science, the latter must be excluded. But unfortunately matters are not always so clear.

It is clear that any program of value exclusion from science must be predicated from the very outset on two indispensable presuppositions: (1) that it is possible to draw a clear line of distinction between statements of fact and judgment of value, and (2) that inference across the boundary between these—and in particular the demonstration of judgment of value from statements of fact—is inherently impossible. But it is not difficult to see that both of these contentions are very questionable.

WHY FACT/VALUE SEPARATION IS UNTENABLE I: LOGICAL GROUNDS

Considerations of general principle might seem to indicate that evaluative conclusions cannot be derived for purely factual premises. However, a significant stumbling block for all theories of fact-value separation is the seemingly paradoxical circumstance that (1) $F \lor V$ follows deductively from the factual premise F (and thus is itself presumably factual), while nevertheless (2) $F \lor V$ in conjunction with a factual premise (viz. not-F) yields the evaluative conclusion V (and thus is itself presumably evaluative).[2]

The plausible response here is to abandon the idea that the logical consequence of factual statements must always be factual, and proceed to class $F \lor V$ as hybrid rather than strictly or purely factual. This done, we would continue to hold to the principle that evaluative statements never fallow from purely factual ones. But on this basis, one would then have to shift from a two-sided fact/value dichotomy to a tripartite division of statements as factual, evaluative, and *hybrid*, and this muddies the water. For the categories of fact and value are now seen as separated not by a sharp boundary line but by a broad corridor.

WHY FACT/VALUE SEPARATION IS UNTENABLE II: PRACTICAL GROUNDS

Consider the following inference:

All automobiles are man-made
Therefore: All good automobiles are man-made

The premise of this patently valid inference is clearly factual, and its conclusion is clearly evaluative.[3] Does such an example not refute our thesis that factual premise do not yield evaluative conclusions?

Not quite! For closer analysis shows that what is actually at issue in the preceding inference is an enthymematic syllogism that incorporates an unstated premiss:

All automobiles are man-made
[All good automobiles are automobiles]
All good automobiles are man-made

And here that enthymematic minor premise can (and should) be regarded as an unproblematically acceptable on grounds of its effective triviality.

In cases of this sort, where the gap between factual premises and an evaluative conclusion is so narrow that it can be filled by an evaluative truism we have a situation where the fact/value gap is effectively bridgeable. And the unquestioning acceptance of such theses would seem to be the price of a consistent overall position.

WHAT IS LEFT OF VALUE-FREEDOM?

It is sometimes maintained that evaluative statements cannot figure in science because they are, by their very nature, neither true nor false. But this is simply nonsense. That it is foolish never to seek the advice of a knowledgeable person, and it is ill-advised to prefer a product one deems inferior to an equally available alternative that one sees as superior. And yet such evaluative claims are clearly every bit as true as the claim that grass is generally green. Such statements obviously state facts—only evaluative facts. (Yet another nail in the coffin of an insuperable fact/value divide!) One must avoid the confusion of *values* and *tastes*. "There's no disputing about *tastes*" may be true, but "There's no disputing about *values*" certainly is not. Values too can be altogether objective, in that value claims admit of rational substantiation—through impersonally cogent considerations. And this circumstance renders it deeply problematic to maintain that the scientist qua scientist must refrain from drawing the normative conclusions that emerge from the facts at his disposal.

It should, however, be acknowledged that there is one important respect in which the advocates of scientific value-neutrality have it right. For what is correct is not that social sciences are altogether value free, but that any policy recommendations regarding social arrangements should be clear and explicit about the values that supposedly militate for its acceptance. The idea is not to keep value out, but make their role overt and explicit insofar as they enter in: there should be no hidden agenda, concealed interest, correct aim, etc.

In the final analysis, however, there is something decidedly self-inconsistent about any such advocacy of value exclusion from science. For of course the only possible justification of this contention would issue from a premiss along such lines as "Staking evaluative claims in the social sciences is inappropriate because doing so does disservice to the prospects of realizing the proper aims of the enterprise—viz. achieving a deepened explanatory understanding of social phenomena." But the fusion of factual and evaluative considerations in this claim itself is unmistakable on the very surface of it.

So here too a concept audit with its attention to the conceptual properties clarify both the rationale for and the limits of a significant philosophical doctrine—in this instance that of the putative value freedom of scientific inquiry. For value has established a secure beachhead not only with respect to issues of the *use* of scientific finding but even with respect to the quality of scientific work itself.

NOTES

1. See, for example, his *Der Sinn der Wertfreiheit* (*Logos*, Vol. VII, 1917).

2. This difficulty was first noted by George Mavrodes. See his essay "On Deriving the Normative from the Non-Normative" in the *Papers of the Michigan Academy of Arts and Sciences*, vol. 53 (1968), pp. 353–365.

3. Observe that the statement "Dogs chase only nice cats" combined with the factual theses "Fido is a cat" and "No dog chases Fido" entails the clearly evaluative conclusion "Fido is not a nice cat."

#28

Personhood and Obligation

HUMANS VERSUS PERSONS

Philosophers of many persuasions—including personalists, phenomenologists, existentialists, and others—have stressed the centrality of the human person as a focus of philosophical concern. But while they have dealt extensively with what persons can and should do to the decidedly problematic neglect of just exactly what persons *are*. Against this background is it not only desirable but actually necessary to undertake a proper audit of the conception of personhood.

Since classical antiquity philosophers have taught that man is a rational animal. But does the reverse hold as well: is rational animality invariably humanoid? Here on earth it is perhaps so. But in general, like it or not, the answers is very possibly negative.

Being human is to belong to a particular biological species: *Homo sapiens.* It is a biological category determined by evolutionary considerations. Humans exist only here on earth. However, to be a *person* is something quite different and far broader. It is a functional category determined by one's capacities and modes of thought and action. Persons are intelligent agents that make their way in the world by means of thought, acting on the basis of their beliefs and choices. In principle alien creatures very different from humans could be persons. Thought-implementation—the capacity to act in response to and under the direction of thought is the crux of personhood. Being human defines ones place in the organic scheme of things, but being a person is different from that: it involves the capacity for modes of thought and action that could—in theory—function outside the biological realm as usually understood. Accordingly, personhood is not a biological but a functional status, and carries with it not only cognitive but also has ethical and social ramifications. There is

119

no reason of principle why nonhuman organisms (aliens) or purely spiritual creatures (angels) or purely mechanical beings (robots) could not have the abilities needed to qualify them as persons.

A person is then a being who can function in certain characteristic ways and goes about doing certain sorts of things. The concept of a "person" is accordingly a complex one that involves many constituent components—both descriptive and normative. All the same, one cannot be more or less of a person. Being a person turns simply on whether or not certain specific requirements are met.

These requirements include

- *intelligence* (securing and processing information)
- *agency* (being able to act: to produce conditions that otherwise could not be)
- *rational agency* (acting purposively in the light of duly validated reasons)
- *reflexivity* (viewing oneself as a thinking being)
- *recognizance* (viewing others as like oneself in the preceding regards)

Personhood accordingly has not just a biological category but also has a social and ethical dimension. Only at a late stage of evolution did the species *Homo sapiens* produce individuals who qualify as persons.

Accordingly, to be a *person* in the full sense of the term is to see oneself as capable of acting in the light of duly appreciated values. Specifically this means that rational beings are bound to value their personhood itself. Accordingly, the evaluative dimension is crucial to the full-fledged conception of a person. To have this conception of oneself is not only to function as a being of a certain kind but to *value* oneself for it—that is, to deem oneself a bearer of value for this very reason.

Interestingly, it does not lie in the concept of a person that one must necessarily have a body. To be sure, one must be able to act, but this agency could in theory be purely mental—involving solely, say, the direct communication between minds through a sympathetic resonance of some sort. In principle it is not necessary for persons to be embodied.

Persons are first and foremost cognitive agents, beings who act on the basis of information and thought. For such beings, skepticism is not an option: a systemic refusal to accept contentions creates a 100 percent assurance of not having the information needed to guide action: by operating an acceptance policy we create at least some chance (different from zero percent) of having needed information guidance. The questions about acceptance policies is not whether, but which. And here the clearly appropriate answer is that which, best we can tell, most closely conforms to the evidence at our disposal, which is, and can be, nothing other than what has come to us in the course of our (past) experience.

Persons are bound to have beliefs about how matters stand in the world, creating for themselves some sort of mental thought-model about its arrangements. And they have certain felt needs and wants that give them an interest in what goes on. On this basis—that is, on the basis of their beliefs and their interests—they make choices. Their thought encompasses beliefs about the real and about possible as well as evaluations putting some possibility as preferable to others, in relation to their interests, and they will generally choose actions they believe to produce preferable results. It is this capacity to deploy beliefs, evaluations, and choices into conjoint operation in an endeavor to produce results is what defines them as persons. Agency guided by cognition, evaluation, and choice constitute the heart of the matter. And to be fully a person, a being should not only preside over the aforementioned capabilities of cognitive and practical intelligence (belief, desire, choice) but be conscious and indeed self-conscious thereof.

And so, persons as here conceived are intelligent beings who see themselves as having the capacity for self-controlled choice implementation and insist on viewing themselves (and according to the rest of us) as as free and responsible agents who when they act generally "*could* have acted otherwise" in the specific sense that they *would* have acted otherwise if some difference in the circumstances would have motivated them to do so. (The explanatory unravelling of this "if" clause is a very long story, for whose telling the present occasion is not the most suitable.) Accordingly, personhood involves autonomy and self-direction as beings for whom conscious wants and preferences—rather than mere instincts and urges alone—provide the determinants of action.

Being a person calls for seeing oneself as a bearer of value and a possessor of rights. And it is therefore something that generalizes to others. Whatever it is that makes me valuable and deserving will have to do likewise for others as well. In demanding respect and care for ourselves as persons we acknowledge a responsibility to care for the personhood of others. We commit to a special responsibility toward them. In sum our self-classification as persons involves us in a social solidarity which has a moral agenda of rights and responsibilities.

A full-fledged conception of personhood can develop only in a social context. To regard oneself as a possessor of worth and a bearer of rights *in virtue of being a person* is thereby to accord a certain status to persons in general. It is to see persons-in-general as occupying a special place in the scheme of things—as constituting a special category of beings with whom one has a particular kinship and toward whom one consequently bears particular responsibilities.

Seeing that personhood involves more than biology, evolution has not made us humans into persons. That was too much to ask for. But it has given us the resources—the facilities and capacities—that are needed for us to be able to function as such. We have made ourselves into persons through the way in which we make use of our evolutionary endowments. The capabilities that define personhood are the product of evolution. They include

- intelligence and rationality
- agency that is reason-guided (and thus free)
- consciousness and especially self-consciousness

Animals—and especially higher primates—possess some of these capacities certainly intelligence (at a lower level) and possibly free agency (or one that is lower yet). Self-consciousness did not emerge until humanoid evolution was well along. In all these matters exact boundaries are difficult to determine and may well not exist given the conceptual complexity of the transitions involved.

THE SOCIAL AND ETHICAL DIMENSION

We are born *humans* (members of the species *Homo sapiens*), but become *persons*. Only as we progress through childhood and learn to think of ourselves as responsible agents—intelligent-free individuals interacting with others as such—do we become full-fledged persons. (No doubt this communal development reflects a tendency that evolutionary processes have programmed into our developmental history, so that personhood is *de facto* more closely affixed to humanity than abstract theory alone suggests.) Personhood does not represent a biological mode of existence within organic nature, but a social mode of existence within an environing culture. Personhood thus has an inextricably social dimension. The conception of a (full-fledged) person is subject to a principle of reciprocity-expectation.

Being a person then is a matter of having certain capacity—of possessing the ability to function in a certain sort of way. And this raises the question of diminished status. Are small children or mentally deprived or insane people persons? Are people who see themselves as mechanisms or as puppets lacking free will (Spinoza, say, or J. O. de La Mettrie) persons? This is a complex and convoluted issue. But the short answer is yes—for it is in order for other persons to attribute to them a potential or capacity that they currently neither exhibit nor claim for themselves.

To qualify as a person oneself involves acknowledging and accepting as such the other creatures who seem plausibly qualified as being persons. And it involves the expectation that they will reciprocate. In deeming others to be persons, and thereby as entitled to being valued as such—qualified to have me treat *their* interests, their rights and concerns, as deserving *my* respect—I also expect them to see me in exactly this same light. Consequently, if others whom I recognize as persons treat me as a mere thing, and not as a person, it injures my own personhood; it undermines my ability to see myself as a person.

William James says somewhere that we become moral beings only when we believe that we are free agents, because only then will we deliberate about our actions with a view to reasons and thereby function as morally responsible for them. But the real point here is a more fundamental one. It is precisely because persons as such form part of a mutually recognizant community of rational agents that persons are *ipso facto* beings who fall within the domain of morality. (Morality does not inherently root in a social compact. If extraneous persons were to come upon the scene, perhaps from outer space, we would at once have certain moral obligations to one another—to respect one another's "rights" as persons, and the like—which would certainly not need to be products of a prior "agreement" issue sort, real or tacit.)

What is necessary is a move from biological evolution in nature to ethical evolution in thought. In seeing ourselves as persons we lay claim to special status defined by the capacities involved. We profoundly value our personhood, and would rather lose our right arm than our personality. To cease being the persons we are is a version of annihilation. We naturally regard our personhood as a possession of paramount value. And because we make this claim for ourselves—if our personhood is to count as having paramount value—then we must also concede this special status to similarly endowed others. And in conceding them such status we stand committed to a special responsibility for care and concern. If personhood is a condition of paramount value that we prize greatly in ourselves, than it has to be in itself—whenever it is encountered.

On this basis, personhood carries in its wake a moral sense of right—of obligation, fairness and justice in relation to other persons. Personhood is thus a conditions of profound ethical involvements.

Due care for the interest of other persons—morality in short takes root in a personhood itself. For if one is a person who recognizes and prizes this very fact, then one ought for that very reason to behave morally by taking the interests of other such beings into account. For if I am (rationally) to pride myself on being a rational agent, then I must stand ready to value in other rational agents what I value in myself—that is, I must deem them *worthy* of respect, care, etc. in virtue of their status as such. What is at issue is not so much a matter of *reciprocity* as one of *rational coherence* with claims that one does—or, rather, should—stake for oneself. For to see myself in a certain normative light I must, if rational, stand ready to view others in the same light. If we indeed are the sort of intelligent creature whose worth in its own sight is a matter of prizing something (reflective self-respect, for example), then this item by virtue of this very fact assumes the status of something we are bound to recognize as valuable—as deserving of being valued. In seeing ourselves as *persons*—as free and responsible rational agents—we thereby rationally bind ourselves to a care for one another's interests insofar as those others too are seen as having this status.[1]

Concept auditing encounters special problem with personhood. For here the relevant issues come too close to home. The reciprocal entanglement of conceptual and philosophical considerations is so intricate and complex in this context that the usual separation between philosophical and pre-philosophically philological considerations cannot readily be implemented.

NOTE

1. To be sure, someone may ask: "Why think ourselves in this way—why see ourselves as free rational agents?" But of course to ask this is to ask for a good rational reason and is thus already to take a stance within the framework of rationality. In theory, one can of course "resign" from the community of rational beings, abandoning all claims to being more than "mere animals." But this is a step one cannot *justify*—there are no satisfactory rational grounds for taking it. And this is something most of us realize instinctively. The appropriateness of acknowledging others as responsible agents whenever possible holds in our own case as well.

Control Issues

CONTROL

The idea of control affords examples of a concept whose scrutiny rivals unexpected complications. It is particularly instructive because the conception of being in control has multiple philosophical involvements, and arises in a wide variety of philosophical contexts. It plays a significant role in moral philosophy and in jurisprudence, in setting limits to responsibility since one of the standard ways of rebutting blame or defeating recrimination is by establishing that what happened occurred "due to circumstances beyond one's control." It is important in philosophical psychology, because of its role in the characterization of action, since an action that one does—in contradistinction to something that one "just happens" to do (such as a reflex reaction) is an item of behavior over whose occurrence one exercises control. It is involved in the logic of commands and imperatives, because a proper command cannot require of its addressee a response that does not lie within his control. And finally, the conception of control is important in the philosophy of science: in describing the workings of physical systems it is important to distinguish between the dependent and the independent variables of the equations descriptive of their mode of functioning, that is, between those (controlling) parameters which are basic in the causal situation because their variation initiates change, and on the other hand those (controlled) parameters which respond to variations in the former.[1] More important yet, an understanding of this concept is bound up with a clear conception of the very nature of science—for it is a commonplace that "control over nature" is one of the definitive tasks of the scientific enterprise, and, to be clear about this, one must obviously first understand just what control is all about. It is thus clear that the idea of control has a prominent place in a widely differentiated group of philosophical settings.

But what is control? Consider some of the items over which a person may exercise control: the ballerina over the position of her limbs, the swimmer over his breath, the pianist over his instrument, the pilot over his aircraft, the drill sergeant over his platoon. Control is varied: people may be in control of instruments of themselves (their bodies), of other people. But in all these cases there is the common core of power to produce desired results that is characteristic of control.

In general terms, control—full control—is the capacity to intervene in the course of events so as to be able both to make something happen and to preclude it from happening, this result being produced in a way that can be characterized as in some sense intended or planned or foreseen. Control thus calls for the possibility of causal participation ("intervention")[2] in the course of events ("to make something happen or preclude it") which can be exercised both positively ("to make happen") and negatively ("to preclude from happening"). Control is a matter of potential, of capability or capacity. Thus, the usual distinction between potentiality and actuality must be maintained. What the controller can do if he chooses is the essential consideration. This explains the aptness of the locution "He thought he had control over R, but he didn't." The difference between having control and exercising it must be recognized, the latter being the actualization of the potentiality represented by the former.[3]

When only one part of these two requisite capacities is at hand, we have to do with what is but one incomplete aspect of control. Thus (merely) negative control over a result is the capacity of assuring it's not happening, though possibly not that of assuring its happening. Conversely, (merely) positive control is the capacity of assuring its happening, though possibly not that of assuring its non-happening. A person who can dispose over a necessary condition for a result has negative control over it, and one Who can dispose over a sufficient condition has positive control: for full control both a necessary and a sufficient condition of the result's being realized must be at his disposal.

In control situations a certain tightness of fit between the controller's actions and the controlled result is required. The connection must be systematic and secure. In a physical system (e.g., a light operated by a switch) the needed connecting linkage is underwritten by natural laws. In systems involving humans (e.g., the conductor's control over his orchestra or the sergeant's control over his platoon) the connecting linkage is underwritten by social practices involving laws, regulations, agreements, customs, sanctions, etc. The linkage of necessary and sufficient determinability of control is generally based on physiconomological connections on the one hand or the somewhat larger but still effective connections of the "laws" of social transactions upon the other.

Consider the following apparatus. Suppose a water tank with each of two controllers in charge of one of two separate evacuating spigots, so that Mr. A can regulate the setting of Spigot 1 and Mr. B that of Spigot 2. Note that neither controller has full control over the outflow—that is, over the presence or absence of an outflow. But each exercises negative control over the outflow (i.e., each can, single-handedly, determine that there will not be any outflow). And together they exercise positive control, and therefore they conjointly exercise full control in our specified sense. On one common view of the matter, we have the thesis: If someone can act so as to assure that (the result) R obtains, then he has control over R. But this idea is false according to our specified conception of control; or at any rate, it is a half-truth. For negative (i.e., preclusive) control must also be involved. Whereas the thesis claims full control on the basis of something sufficient to establish solely what we have designated as merely positive control.

It might seem on first thought that the distinction between positive and negative control, being dichotomous, is confined in applicability to control situations of the simple ON-OFF variety of our faucet example. But this is not so. Positive control involves the power to assure a desired result, negative control the power to prevent an undesired result. These pertain also to nondichotomous cases. Consider a dial that can be set on any of a number of positions 1, 2, 3, ... If X presides over a device that prevents the dial's assuming any given position—without, however, stopping it at certain predictable settings—then X has negative control over the setting of the dial. (We have to suppose that the device works only once on each occasion—so that X cannot simply keep on actuating it until he ultimately gets what he wants.) Again, let the result at issue be "Setting the dial on setting No. 1," and suppose further that (1) the dial gets immovably stuck at this setting, and (2) the dial has an insuperable tendency to slip into this setting of its own accord. Under these assumptions, X will have positive control over the specified result, but will lack negative control over it.

One striking feature of control is that it can be exercised not only over things, but also over other agents, agents distinct from the controller himself. Moreover, it can be exerted at a distance, so that the controller, who determines what the agent will do, and the agent himself, who actually does whatever is being accomplished, are two distinct individuals. The controller himself need exercise no agency whatever, over and above whatever activities are requisite for his exercise of control. Apart from this, all of his "actions" can be vicarious. He can work through intermediaries, mechanical (as in "remote control") or human (as an air traffic controller controls the movements of an aircraft through the pilot).

PARTIAL CONTROL VERSUS FULL CONTROL

Whenever control is exercised conjointly by several controllers (as in the spigot example above) one can say that each controller has partial control, or in such cases one may also speak of "divided concontrol" or "shared control." Partial control may be either positive or negative. If a safe can be opened only if each of three different men makes appropriate settings on distinct dials, then each has full negative control (i.e., each can prevent the safe's opening), but every man has only partial positive control. By way of contrast, if several men all know the combination to the same safe, then each can exercise full positive control over the safe's being open, but each only has partial negative control—since the others can all open it, and negative control only resides in the entire group.

It might seem at first blush that all instances of partial control of something resolve into full control over an associated something else. Not "the door's being open or not" (in the examples of the preceding paragraph), but "the dial's being set on door-open or door-closed position." Or, in the spigot example of Sect. 2, not "water flowing from the faucet" but "the spigot being set on flow-through position."

Consider the idea the possession of partial control (over something) is always correlated with the possession of full control (over an associated something else). This is surely not correct. Our examples have been misleading in this regard because all of them still involve some type of full control over some result R. But consider the following example. Suppose that full control over something is vested in a three man committee under conditions of majority rule. Then its three members all have only partial control—negative or positive alike. Note that now none of the controllers has full control over anything that has to do with R as such. Of course it might be said that each one has full control over "how he exercises such control as he does have"—that is, in the present example, each one has control over "his own vote." But to save the thesis by bringing this mode of "control" upon the tapis, is to save it at the cost of a substantial evisceration. For the "associated something else" over which the controller exercises full control (viz., how he marks his ballot) is in such cases "associated" with the controlled item (say, the building of a dam) in so remote and tenuous a way as to empty the thesis at issue to point of trivialization.

INFLUENCE

It is important to draw a distinction between partial control on the one hand, and what I propose—somewhat arbitrarily—to term influence upon the other.[4] Essential in the idea of control is a condition of definiteness: the controller(s) can definitely make something happen or definitely preclude its happening. But there is also the prospect of what by way of contrast with control—we shall call influence, viz., the capacity to make something's happening more likely or less likely. For example, the taking of vitamin pills may render it less probable that I shall contract a common cold. The pills do not give me control—not even incomplete control—over my catching colds: the connection is merely one of influence in the specified sense (i.e., taking the pill "influences" whether or not I shall catch cold). When partial control is shared with a great number of other (partial) controllers, so that the aspect of control is very thinly attenuated, it is plausible to regard the matter in the light of influence rather than in terms of control. (An example of this would be that of a voter in a very large electorate.) A paradigm example of the contrast can be given in terms of a "fixed" roulette wheel in a gambling house. We should speak of "control" if the house can select the specific outcome of the wheel, but if the house can merely affect the probability-distribution of the outcome, without being able to determine any specific outcome, we should—in our terminology—have to speak of "influence" (rather than control).

It might be objected: "You have no right to deny the rubric of 'control' to what you call 'influence'. This is merely a matter of somewhat arbitrary verbal legislation." We reply: To some extent a decision about the use of words is involved, going beyond the mere explanation of existing usages. But the decision is not an arbitrary one—it has a basis in a genuine distinction based on a difference that has to be reckoned with in any event. We thus reply to the objector: "You are certainly free to apply to our 'influence' some such label as 'weak control'. What counts is the distinction at issue—which now for you becomes that between weak and strong control-the terminology is largely immaterial."

Although we have drawn a sharp distinction between influence and control, it should be recognized that the (deliberate) exercise of influence invariably involves doing something over which one has control (e.g., taking the cold pills), so that the actual *use* of this influence will have to be something over which one has control.

One lesson of these deliberations is the incorrectness of the oft-maintained contention that it is only when we have outright contact that we are only morally responsible in relation to outcome. Clearly the exercise of exerting mere influence will also incur some degree of responsibility.

DIRECT CONTROL VERSUS INDIRECT CONTROL

We are tempted to say that one has direct control over the light switch, the steering wheel, and the key, but only indirect control over the light, the

wheels of the car, and the lock. The distinction here at issue must be scruti-
nized. We must see whether there is a distinct category of control situations
where the exercise of control is direct.

Just how would one characterize this matter of direct control? The best
approach to the question proceeds by way of the distinction between direct
and indirect control. Perhaps this distinction is to be drawn in this way—that
one controls directly what one manipulates with one's hands or other parts of
the body, and indirectly whatever is controlled as a causal consequence of the
exercise of direct control. But this conception of directness is highly problematic. Is direct control only exercised in immediate bodily contact? What about
the person who wears gloves, or even whose hand is covered by a film of oil?
And over what is this "immediate contact" variety of direct control exercised?
Is only that part of the steering wheel in touch with one's hands manipulated
directly and the rest of the wheel indirectly?

Moreover one would have to construe "manipulation" here in terms of
intentional bodily movement. But even this will not serve. For what if I move
my one hand, held limp (or suppose-paralyzed) with the other. Now if I push
a stone along with my limp hand it is certainly "moved by a bodily contact
resulting from an intentional bodily movement"—and thus the motion would be
directly controlled on the definition at issue (unlike the case in which I push the
stone along with my gloved hand when motion would be controlled indirectly!).

Accordingly, the distinction between the causal and the intentional order
is an important one. Of the traffic light gone berserk, we may still say that it
"regulates"—or, as we said above, "determines"—the traffic in some way—
"controlling" it in the causal order, even though it is no longer "under control" in the intentional order.

MODUS OPERANDI

Consider two piles of stones A and B—and suppose a controller to exercise
control over:

the relative size of A and B.

The controller can thus determine, *ex hypothesi*, whether $A > B$, $B > A$, or
$A = B$. Here control is in its role of a selection-mechanism. We have a system
(the two piles) which can be in several alternative states:

$(S_1)A > B,$

$(S_2) B > A,$

$(S_3) A = B$

And the controller is in the position to select (determine, "control") which state the system is to be in. But this, of course, is not the whole story. It Wholly leaves out of account the issue of the modus operandi: the issue of the means and manner (processes, procedures, techniques, control devices, etc.) by which the controller effects his selection of one of these alternatively realizable states of the system under his control.

For even after all of the preceding considerations have been settled, the question remains: How are we to suppose the controller exercises his control? There are four basic possibilities: The controller may be able

(1) To add stones to A.
(2) To take stones from A.
(3) To add stones to B.
(4) To take stones from B.

These four items spell out the modus operandi at issue, by specifying where the "points of control" lie at which the controller intervenes to exercise his mode of control. The modus operandi in this control situation is determined by the exact combination of these four basic modes of control-exercising capabilities we may assume to lie within the controller's power. Thus knowledge of the modus operandi enables us to specify the independent and the dependent "variables" (i.e., parameters at issue in the control situation).

The modus operandi is an important, integral part of the control situation. A command, for example, may well be such that its recipient is not only directed to bring to realization a certain result-state in a matter over which he has control, but may also lay down the modus operandi—specifying the way (means, manner, timing, etc.) by which this result is to be achieved.[5]

WHAT CAN BE UNDER ONE'S CONTROL?

It would appear on first sight that many sorts of things can be under one's control. The beginning of a list might be as follows: other people, instruments and instrumentalities, states of affairs (e.g., the setting of a dial), and the realization of a proposition (e.g., whether "The light is on" is to be true or false).

Consider the following set-up. In a room with an uncurtained window there is a lighting fixture worked by a switch over which Mr. X exercises complete control. The question now arises: Does Mr. X control the quantity of illumination in the room? He certainly does not have full control over this. Nor does he have partial control in our technical sense of control sharing since he does not share full control with any other controllers (but at best with the sun and moon). Nor is the matter a probabilistic one, so that the situation cannot be described in terms of influence in our technical sense.

But still, undeniably, Mr. X is in a position to affect decisively and alter systematically the quantity of illumination at issue. How then is this to be put in terms of control? Quite simply as follows: Mr. X controls the quantity of extra-natural illumination in the room ("extra natural" illumination in the sense of that apart from whatever illumination is provided by sunlight or moonlight). Thus to make our terminology applicable we have to shift the specification of what it is that is controlled away from "the quantity of illumination in the room." For with respect to this item this control parameter as I shall call it—Mr. X exercises neither control nor influence, according to the construction we have placed upon these conceptions.

But this example does present a situation we have not heretofore considered—namely that of full control of a certain component or constituent of an aggregate result. For this case we may introduce the terminology of fragmentary control. The man who writes on a moving train controls his pencil in this fragmentary way—the pencil moves in part according to the willed movements of his hand and fingers (over which he has control) and in part according to the lurchings of the train (with which he has nothing to do). Fragmentary control is another mode of control that is incomplete or "partial" in a broader sense, in addition to the particular type of partial (i.e., shared) control considered above. The controller who, as it were, "shares" his control not with other controllers but with "natural forces" may be said to be in fragmentary control over the result at issue, provided that his role in its realization is a sufficiently prominent one.

Control must always have an object, but it invariably relates to an aspect of this object as for example:

the location of the patient
the position of the door
the setting of a dial
the orientation of one's hand
the pointing of a pencil

Of course a controller may exercise control over several aspects of a controlled object. Whenever we say that X is in control of a thing or that the thing is "under X 's control," it is always in fact such partial or aspective power over this thing that is at issue. In this context we may introduce the idea of "degrees of freedom" in control over an object to designate the various (independent) respects in which the controlled object is in the controller's power.

OBLIGATION AND CONTROL

It is a doctrine widely accepted among philosophers over the ages that moral obligation presupposes control—that we are only ever to be praised or blamed for matters with respect to which we are fully in control. Accordingly it is held that one deserves neither approbation or reprehension for doing something that one cannot avoid doing.

However, it has been argued in opposition to this doctrine that it is invalidated by counterexamples such as the following.

- Let us suppose that I really dislike you. And let it be that I learn that some misfortune has befallen you. I greet this news with gladness and rejoicing. This response is automatic and uncontrollable. And yet it is surely wrong and reprehensible.

Or again:

- Let us suppose that you and I are rivals on some way—for recognition by our boss, say, or even simply as brothers linked by the not uncommon phenomenon of sibling rivalry. And let it be that some sort of good fortune comes your way. I am deeply annoyed by this—literally green with envy. And this reaction is one that I really cannot help—I do not choose to make it: it is an automatic "knee jerk" reaction. And yet it is not just regrettable that I should so respond, but actually reprehensible. (I "ought to be ashamed of myself"—and perhaps even am.)

However, close attention to the nature of such counterexamples is revealing in its indication of an underlying principle. For their bearing is not upon the *actions* of people but their *reactions*: their concern is not with what people actively do, but rather with how they passively respond. And that sort of thing is of course something that is usually outside of our control. And in view of this construal those purported counterexamples actually misfire.

Moreover, there are also other examples which suggest that control is not presupposed for moral obligation. Suppose that X is kept from falling into an abyss by three ropes held by A, B, and C, any two of which suffice to secure X. It would clearly be incorrect of A to reason: "Holding this rope is a hard task. I might as well let it go. After all, whether or not X falls is not upon me. Nothing I do settles the matter one way or the other." But despite X's lack of actual control, this proceeding would surely be reprehensible. However, it could now be replied that while A is not guilty of having X fall, something that he does not control, he is indeed guilty of *needlessly putting X at a risk of falling*, something that he does indeed control.

MORAL COMPLICATIONS

All in all, it be acknowledged that control is a complex matter. Consider the hypothetical supposition that I am to determine whether or not a certain pill will be added to X's breakfast meal—a pill which, I am led to believe, is an antidote to a poison in X's system which will otherwise kill him. Do I direct adding that pill? Let it be that in actual fact, while X is indeed poisoned that pill is a totally ineffectual bread pellet. Giving it to X will have no effect—he is doomed. So while I indeed control the administration of the pill, I exert no control whatsoever over the outcome. Just where does this leave matters from the moral point of view?

One key point to note is that given what I take myself to know it would be reprehensible for me not to have the pill administered. And this consideration means that the moral status of my act is not a matter of the actual outcome (where *ex hypothesi* I exercise no control): the fact that I see myself as having control will suffice.

And the next salient consideration is that what is paramount for moral assessment is the *envisioned and intended* outcomes; not the actual reality of things but the envisioned reality of the agent's though-world. And here we indeed are in control—or at any rate see ourselves as being so.

If I play Russian roulette with your life I do not control the outcome, but clearly act in a morally reprehensible way. On the other hand, suppose that I do in fact control the outcome. This by itself does not provide for moral responsibility, seeing that this requires something over and above mere control as such, namely that this control be exercised, and both knowingly and voluntarily. And even when I have control over a negative outcome I do not necessarily bear any moral responsibility. Jones, Smith's bitter enemy, has him at gunpoint and is about to shoot him. I stand near the line of fire and can readily interpose myself and "take the bullet" for Smith. Whether or not Smith gets shot is effectively within my control. And yet I bear no moral responsibility here. Interposing myself to save Smith would be an act of supererogation and not withstanding my control, in letting matters take their course I bear no responsibility for Smith's injuries both knowingly and voluntarily.

So here again we have a case where a concept audit produces a positive result. But now rather than serving to invalidate a philosophically contentious theory, a concept audit guards it against an ultimately untenable line of objection.

NOTES

1. For example, when applying Boyle's gas law $P = T \times V$ in the usual piston-in-cylinder case, is the piston being held fixed and the cylinder being heated (V : constant. T = the independent variable, P = the dependent variable). Or is the piston being drawn out with the temperature kept constant (T = constant, V = the independent variable, P = the dependent variable)?

2. The concept of intervention is a complicated one, but we shall not stop to explicate it here. What is principally at issue is a long story regarding the formula of "how things would have gone but for. . . ."

3. It must be noted that control (positive or negative) may be exercised in some cases not so much by any "action" as by inaction, omission, and inactivity (e.g., a failure to exercise a veto).

4. Our use of this term is technical—it has only a remote connection with the standard usage of one person's having influence with (over, upon) another. In ordinary usage, when X can get Y to do what he wants, he may be said to influence Y if the means by which he does this are friendship, cooperation, and permission; but he will be said to control Y if the means include threats, pains, or penalties. Here the difference between control and influence is made to turn on the agent's motivation. He acts in response to the controller's instructions because of such-and-such considerations. The difference between influence and control is made to turn on the nature of these considerations.

5. A modus operandi under the heading of means (rather than manner) may be lacking in those control situations which we have characterized as noninstrumental in Sect. 7 above.

#30

Fairness Problems

EGALITARIANISM ISSUES

Egalitarianism is one of those ideas which, like time or romantic love, one understands well enough until one stops to think closely about it.

In the eyes of God everything—and certainly everyone—is significant, seeing that "not even a sparrow falls but the Father takes note of it."[1] And egalitarians, so we are told, are people who desire that everybody should be treated in the same way. "Treat everyone alike!" is their motto.

But surely nobody really thinks this. Who would desire that one's spouse or one's physician should treat everyone just the same. Surely not everyone has equal needs and requirements in matters of treatment—the parent as well as the stranger, the employer as much as the passerby.

"But that's not what is meant," we will be told. "The proper concern for egalitarianism is not the private individual, but the agent who represent the state in some official capacity."

But is this any better? Should the judge treat everyone the same, be they guilty or innocent? Should the tax man impose the same exactions upon the rich and the poor? Should the drivers' licensing bureau be indifferent as between those aged nine and nineteen or as between the sighted and the vision-impaired?

In the face of these issues, the following sort of objection might be raised: "All this overlooks what is the core of egalitarianism—the doctrine of equality before the law." But this defense has its problems. Should the law really impose the same penalties on the robber and the robbed, the mugger and his victim? "Of course not—you misunderstand. What is wanted is that the law should grant no unearned advantages and impose no unmerited disadvantages." But what of the differential treatment of juveniles and adults; or of the native born versus the naturalized citizens in the case of the U.S. Presidency?

"But this sort of complaint also misses the point," says egalitarianism's exponent. "What is wanted is only that everyone should be treated the same as everyone else *who is in the same circumstances*." The operative principle is (or should be) not "Treat everyone alike" but rather "Treat like cases alike." On this basis, what the egalitarian's idea of equal treatment has in view is going to be pervasively contextualized. At best the maxim will have to be "Don't allow something to make a difference that doesn't involve there being a difference in some issue-relevant respect!" And this is not so much a doctrine as a trivial truism.

At the core of distributive fairness, then, lies the demand for an equality of outcomes in the face of an equality of claims, and, more generally for a coordination of outcomes with the magnitude of claims. The defining idea is that of giving people their proper due (*suum cuique tribuere* in the classical formula). Even small children have an acute sensitivity to issues of fairness. The cry of an aggrieved participant in a playground game "Now it's my turn—it's just not fair to leave me out" is only too familiar.

With fairness, four interrelated but nevertheless distinct conceptions will come into play:

Equal distribution: an allocation of the same amount to each qualified claimant.

Correct distribution: an allocation in strict alignment with the claims of the claimants, each recipient getting exactly is *equal* to his claim.

Claim-proportionate distribution: an allocation in line with the claims of the recipients: each gets what is *proportionate* to his claim.

Equitable distribution: an allocation which treats one claimant more favorably than another whenever—but only when—his claims are stronger.

It is clear that rather different and distinct conceptions of fairness are at work with those preceding specifications. For example, neither is an even-division procedure that treats all claimants alike necessarily fair (i.e., claim-proportionate)—nor, conversely, need the fair thing to do be egalitarian in this way. (Otherwise it would not make sense to distinguish between gold, solver, and bronze medals.) Those different conceptions of fairness operate differently. There can certainly be situations in which all four of these coincide. But this of course would be a very special case.

All four of these modes of fairness contrast with yet another relevant conception:

Just distribution: an allocation to recipients according to what is, all considered appropriate ("right and proper") in the prevailing circumstances.

Note that throughout this range, all of the conditions at issue are comparative in nature, relating to how one claimant is treated in comparison with others.

Consider an illustrative situation. Aunt Mary's entire estate consists of two oil paintings, a fine landscape by Cezanne and a mediocre portrait of Uncle John by a comparative unknown. Her two nephews Bob and Bill are the joint and equal heirs. They agree that Bob gets the Cezanne and Bill the Uncle John, to which he attributes great sentimental value—he would gladly buy it for twice what the Cezanne will bring at auction. In point of monetary value Bob makes a killing, in point of subjective value Bill does so. What is one to say about the distribution? Clearly it is inequitable (by any standard). Nor is it fair, since fairness is a matter of objectivity, and when objectively rather that subjectively valued, those shares are decidedly unequal. Nevertheless, each party is perfectly satisfied. Clearly objective fairness is one thing and claimant-satisfaction another. Inequitable though it is, the postulated division is perfectly just.

Is it unfair to tax the high earner more than the low? It is all a matter of the standards of claim assessment. If we look not at the *amount* of the tax, but to its *proportion*, then taxing the earner of $100 by $10 is just the same as taxing the earner of $1000 by $100 since in both cases alike we tax the individual 10% of income. And if—as classic economic theory has it—the marginal utility of money decreases with the amount in hand, then that $10 from $100 (i.e., 10%) may be equated to $100 in $1000 (i.e., 10%), so a graduated tax that increases the percentage take in line with the amount earned looks to be perfectly fair.

Claim proportionality is a pivotal factor with fairness. Consider the problem of affording the credit for a discovery. For the sake of example, let it be that three particular inquirers (A, B, C) address a problem whose theoretically possible answers occupy the following solution space (Figure 30.1):

1	2	3
4	5	6
7	8	9

Figure 30.1

Now let it be that *A* finds that the correct solution cannot be in the last row, *B* finds that it must lie in the first column, *C* establishes that it is not 1. Among the three of them, they have arrived as 4 as the correct solution. But who gets how much credit? Let the respective fraction of credit be *a*, *b*, and *c*, so that $a + b + c = 1$. Since *A* and *B* each eliminate just 6 possibilities we have it that $a = b$. Since *c* eliminates just one possibility we have $6c = b = a$. We now have three equations in three unknowns, and thereby find the resultant solution to be: $a = 6/13$, $b = 6/13$, $c = 1/13$. Just this allocation proportions the credit of each party to the comparative size of their contribution, and accordingly establishes the fair allocation of credit. *A* and *B* each get a bit less than half, and *C* the rest. (Of course, this analysis presupposes that are equal effort—in terms of time, resources, ingenuity, etc.—is required the elimination of the individual possibilities.)

In circumstances where the realization of a fair distribution is infeasible (on grounds such as individuality, for example), an effort at approximating fairness can always be made by affording the effected parties with an equality of opportunity by resolving to a probabilistic division. In this way the impracticality of achieving a fairness of result can be atoned for by guarding for a fair distribution of probabilities. Thus when *A*'s claim to an indivisible good is twice as strong as *B*'s, one might resort to allocating that good with *A*'s probability of winning twice that of *B*.

FAIRNESS AND CLAIMS

There are many sorts of claim-creating events: some natural (children born), some culturally conventional (races won), many legal (marriages made, children adopted, deeds of gift executed, lotteries won). These can and do create claims where none existed before. The creation of such claims can be wise or unwise, just or unjust, proper or improper. But they cannot be fair or unfair. Only in the presence of *pre-existing* claims does fairness come into it: where there are no claims there is no place for fairness either.

This circumstance means, among other things, that while we must acknowledge that nature does not deal with people equally in regard to people's condition of birth—clearly, for example, in relation to medical issues—we cannot say that nature is unfair.

And other relevant considerations arise in this regard. For there are two modes of inequality: viz. those inequalities instituted by nature and those instituted by man. Nature's inequalities are not redistributable—good looks, intelligence, personal congeniality, etc. are distributed by fate in ways largely impervious to human intervention. But the man-made inequalities that inhere in legal or social arrangements can often be ameliorated. Yet sometimes not.

It may be regrettable that someone already wealthy should win the lottery, but there is nothing unfair about it. In a heavily Hispanic voting district the odds may be tilted in an otherwise undeserved way in favor of an Hispanic candidate, but there is nothing unfair about it.

It is certainly inequitable that some should be born into rich families and others into poor, that some should be handsome and others ugly, some talented and others inept. But there is nothing unfair or unjust about it. For there must be prior, pre-established claims if concepts of fairness and justice are to gain traction. It may be regrettable that Aunt Mirabelle should leave her fortune to a home for stray cats rather than to her good nephew Murgatroyd, but there is nothing unfair about it. After all, it did not do violence to the nephew's just claims upon her estate, seeing that he really didn't have any.

Again, while perhaps regrettable, it is not unfair of Mary to marry John (who is somewhat lukewarm about her) rather than Jim (who loves her ardently). For neither suitor has any pre-existing claim upon her. But does this not mean their claims are equal. By no means! "But my claims are just as good as his." Not really. For this contention is inappropriate where there just are no claims at all. It is like saying his castle is just as grand as mine or his children just as talented as mine in circumstances where neither of us have any. Where there are no valid claims questions of fairness do not arise.

The right and proper claims of individuals comprise their *desert* in the matter of issues. Regrettably, in a difficult and uncooperative world it often transpires that it is not feasible for people to get what they disserve—be it for good or for ill. So here fairness becomes a matter of suboptimization.

The conditions that complicate the issue of fairness are primarily two: a scarcity of resources, and the contingencies of fate. With a scarcity of resources it may be impossible to give everyone their just due. And with the inequities of a fate will often render the conditions of a desert-responsive fairness are often unrealizable.

FAIRNESS VERSUS JUSTICE

Considerations of fairness are predicated on the prevailing claims. But what if those claims themselves arise in a way that is problematic and questionable? Can claims themselves come into existence unfairly, or does justice and fairness come into it only after claims are established?

Claims can certainly originate in ways that seem inappropriate or even unjust: consider primogeniture for example, or the dispositions of an eccentric testator. In the end such arrangements can be problematic in point of reasonableness or even justice. But not in point of fairness as such. For seeing that they originate claims they do not violate preexisting ones. In consequence, while they may originate them in ways that are unjust or unreasonable, but no in ways that are unfair. To reemphasize: In careful usage the language of fairness in specific must not be confounded with the language of justice at large.

It is important to distinguish between fairness regarding process and regarding product. When an indivisible good is controlled to one of two claimants by a coin-toss the process is altogether fair but the product, which leaves one claimant empty-handed, certainly is not. And what this means is that a distribution that is unfair may nevertheless not be unjust.

There are situations in which it is questionable if a fair distribution is automatically also just. For one thing fairness may run afoul of need. It is certainly fair when the law distributes the estate of an intestate decedent equally among his children, but if one of them—unlike the rest—is handicapped and unable to earn a livelihood this may not qualify as altogether just. It is fair to divide television coverage equally between two rival candidates for public office, but if one of them also has a virtually exclusive access to print media then fairness with respect to television coverage will not be altogether just.

Yet another dilemma of fairness lies in the consideration that there are many circumstances in which a realization of the desideratum of aligning results with claims becomes impossible to achieve because of the inherent incompatibility of the claims at issue. A classic illustration of this situation arises in connection with *equal claims to an indivisible good*. And an analogous situation arises with *any insufficiency of resources for meeting equivalent claims*. Say that someone owes $100 to each of two otherwise equivalent creditors, but has sufficient resources to pay only one of them. Here paying the one would obviously be unfair to the other.

To be sure, one might well at this point proceed by random selection. Given that we cannot achieve an equality of outcome, an equality of opportunity is the best we can realize. The result, which leaves one claimant empty-handed, is certainly not fair. But in the circumstances one must concede that it is just, and one lesson here is that justice and fairness cannot be equated.[2]

A terrorist throws a bomb into a crowded meeting room. The hero who grabs it and pitches it out the window will doubtless realize that some people will be killed or injured in the street below. But far fewer. Those street victims do not deserve their sad fate, and would not have it but for our hero's act. What happens to them is nowise fair. But we cannot think that our hero has acted improperly. He has "done the right thing" in averting an even greater misfortune, though the result is certainly not fair to those involved. His actions do not violate the requirements of justice, but fail to meet those of fairness.

Again, consider a comparable case. There are five poisoned victims. But there are available only 3 grams of the needed antidote effective dosage 1 gram. The only strictly fair procedure is to give each victim 3/5 grams of the antidote. But this makes no sense in the prevailing circumstances. To do the strictly fair thing here would be fully and emphatically inappropriate and indeed unjust. Where equal treatment issues are absolutely the principle "Treat like cases alike": must be put into abeyance.[3] The *actual* world order certainly does not treat people fairly, nor is it necessarily the case that a *just* world order need to do so. Neither equality nor fairness are absolute requisites for justice as properly construed. The misconceptions at issue diverge.

And here lies the larger lesson. Life is going to present situations where achieving the just and appropriate outcome is simply unrealizable, and the best and most that can be achieved is a fair distribution of chances and opportunities. This shift from fair outcomes to fair chances is sometimes the only way to achieve an appropriate surrogate for fairness in various circumstances.

The entry of chance into these deliberations creates problems of its own. The winner of a lottery has a right—a just claim—to the prize. But he has no right to winning the lottery. The lottery itself is a social process for creating a claim where none existed before. There are many such social processes— contracts of all sorts included.

As regards claims upon individuals or groups, is, just, and right that some people should have larger claims on some of the world's goods than others? Of course it is. The tailor who works twice the hours for you deserves twice the wage. The shoemaker who sells you twice as many shoes deserves twice the price.

Equality too is a conception that is not as easy as it seems. For one thing one must distinguish between an equality of distributive *outcomes* and an equality of *opportunity*. Then too there is the issue of whether equality is achieved in terms of equal value (objectively construed) or of equal satisfaction (subjectively construed).

CAN CLAIMS THEMSELVES BE UNFAIR?

Claims are often rooted in social norms and processes, be they legal or customary. But there are moral claims as well as legal or customary ones. In a civilized society people have a moral claim to be treated courteously by others irrespective of what the laws and the customs may be. Such claims root in the very nature of things.

Can legitimate claims be created unjustly? Indeed they can! It may not be right that you should give child *A* twice the birthday presents you give to child *B*, but once the gift has been made their claims are established. For better or for worse, in a society of free agents there is no reason why valid claims cannot issue from inappropriate or even unjust proceedings.

One of the great paradoxes of political philosophy lies in the circumstance that our intuition regarding the legitimating basis of claims involves inner conflicts. For one thing, there is the idea that a person's claims on the world's stock of goods should stand proportionate to his contributions to them. (This is the *value-added* or *productive contribution* perspective.) For another thing the idea that a person's claims on the world's share of goods should stand in proportion to the person's need for such goods—specifically in the case of those who are somehow disadvantaged for reasons not of their own making. (This is the *value needed* or *handicap-offsetting* perspective.) Then too there is the egalitarian idea that everyone's share of the world's goods should be equal: that people should be equal not just before the law but before the world. (This is the *value-shared* or *egalitarian* perspective.) Abstractly speaking, each of these principles has its drawing power. Seemingly, one possible resolution would be to deploy a mixed strategy at this point, one which contemplates attending x percent according to contribution, y percent according to need, and the remaining z percent equally. To be sure, this plausible strategy settles nothing by itself, because the argument regarding the appropriate size is x, y, and z would in theory be endless. But in practice every society has its political system arrive at some sort of resolution, with the result that some are contribution-intensive (e.g., the United States), some are need-intensive (Scandinavia), and some egalitarian (especially those drastically underdeveloped societies which achieve virtual equality by having close to nothing allocate).

MODES OF DISTRIBUTION

Could one perhaps *conjoin* all those different modes of fairness into one and say that a distribution is unqualifiedly fair if it is fair in all of these different senses at once. However, this would not work out in a satisfactory way because those different conceptions so readily conflict with one another.

But though one cannot conjoin them one can take a different, more circumspect combinatory approach.

We may characterize the totality of claims in a given situation as its *claim pool* (P) and the totality of resources available for meeting those claims as the *claim stake* (S). In theory there are three possibilities here, according as $P = S$; $P > S$; $P < S$. The first of these is theoretically the most convenient: here the obviously proper move is simply to meet those claims. The issue of fairness principally arises when $S < P$ and an allocation of loss and disappointment is at hand. This poses interesting questions of procedure.

Now consider the situation of Figure 30.2 where there is an insufficiency for settling the claims. In cases of this sort various divisions can be contemplated each of which implements a different strategy:

(1) Maximal claim satisfaction: minimal disappointment among claimants
(2) Equal allocation of the shortfall of 12 among the three claimants. (Each makes an equal sacrifice of 4.)
(3) Claim-proportionate allocation of the shortfall. (Each claimant losses the same proportion—i.e., 50%.)
(4) Equal distribution among the claimants.

With preferential voting among the claimants, distribution (1) might well prevail. But this seems clearly unjust in view of the sacrifice imposed on *A*. This situation illustrates that democratic procedure is no guarantor of fairness (which is the reason, among others, why the U.S. constitution was supplemented by a Bill of Rights).

With voting eliminated, it emerges that among the remaining three remaining alternatives (3) alone meets the requirement of strict fairness (outcome proportionate to the claim). But (2) and (4) also meet the requirement of equal treatment (i.e., equal sacrifice in Case (2) vs. equal outcome in Case (4)). (Arguably these resolutions would also have some claim on being considered "just.")

At this point we arrive at the prospect of a process egalitarianism:

Whenever a procedural process is at issue in circumstances where considerations of rationality and plausibility leave open several distinct possibilities, then proceed by a mixed strategy which gives *equal scope to all* of the qualified alternatives.

This principle is predicated in the idea that whenever several distinct processes of distribution are equally cogent, it is only reasonable to give them equal play. (Here too the Principles of Sufficient Reason is at work.)

A HYPOTHETICAL SITUATION

A total of 12 units are available for meeting the claims (totaling 24) of three individuals

Claims		Possible distributions			
		(1)	(2)	(3)	(4)
A	14	2	10	7	4
B	6	6	2	3	4
C	4	4	0	2	4

Figure 30.2

Applying this procedure in regard to the three reasonable alternatives (2)–(4) of the Figure 30.2 situation we would have it that A's stance is $(10 + 7 + 1) \div 3 = 7$, B's is $(2 + 3 + 4) \div 3 = 3$, and C's is $(0 + 2 + 4) \div 3 = 2$. A process egalitarian approach would yield exactly the same distribution as procedure (3), a consideration which cannot but be seen as speaking in its favor.

PROBLEMS

It seems that people often think that the terms *just, fair*, and *equal* are more or less equivalent. But as the previous deliberations will indicate this is far from being the case. Once the subtle differences between these conceptions are duly acknowledged, it becomes clear that the appropriate applicability of these characterizations can differ markedly.

As the preceding deliberations have shown, an equal-treatment egalitarianism of distributional *claimants* is a procedure of limited appropriateness and applicability. But an equal treatment egalitarianism of distributional *processes* is something else again—a procedure for whose rational appropriateness there is much to be said under the aegis of a principle of sufficient reason. On this basis, in conditions outcome where distributive fairness is an unachievable process egalitarianism seems to provide the most appropriate, just, and rationally defensible way to proceed.

But now some dark clouds come on the horizon, and a mass of problems opens up. For what sorts of respects are issue-relevant? Clearly only those relating to features that can validate treating one person X differently from another Y. But these are just exactly the considerations that define entitlement and desert—that render it right fitting and proper that X be treated x-wise and Y y-wise. And here the crux seems to be not equality but its contrary—desert.

As this sort of deliberation proceeds, the ideas of equality, sameness, treatment, etc. vanish like the Cheshire Cat and leave behind only the smile of the idea that just laws differentiate only where there is sound reasons for doing so—that the state's administration of official and legal matters ought to be rational. Any linkage to the idea of uniformity of treatment is purely coincidental. The factor of equality ceases to be helpfully applicable and simply drops out of the picture.

But at this point our concept audit brings us to a stage where egalitarianism—duly revised to meet some obvious and inescapable objections—becomes indistinguishable from a doctrine of desert. To all intents and purposes, that egalitarian motto has now come to be shifted from "Treat everyone alike" to "Treat everyone in line with their contextually appropriate claims and deserts." But now nothing remains to differentiate egalitarianism from distributive justice writ large. In the course of introducing the explanations and qualifications needed to make the relevant deliberations viable we have transmuted the issue altogether. For egalitarianism has now morphed into what is no more than reasonable fairness.

And so a concept audit of the topic serves to show that the idea of inter-personal equality is a questionable instrument of political philosophy. The pre-systematic idea of equality/identity/sameness cannot be fitted to the objectives at which political theorists of egalitarian orientation are aiming. There just is no way for them to articulate a viable program of egalitarianism as a distinctive doctrine because the idea of equal treatment as distinct from generic fairness and justice cannot be given any stable and coherent political sense.

NOTES

1. Matthew 10: 29; Luke 12: 7.

2. Is it fair that in American presidential elections the candidate who carries a state by 0.01 percent of the vote should get 100 percent of that state's representation in the Electoral College? The answer is an emphatic *yes*—exactly because the claims at issue are legal claims and just this is what the law provides for. But the question "Is it just?" is something else again.

3. But not totally. Those differentiated cases should be selected at random, so that while equality of treatment goes out the window, equality of opportunity does not.

The Ethics of Delegation

THE BASIC IDEA

The question of the extent to which a delegator bears moral responsibility for the actions (and omissions) of a duty delegated representation is one of the many knotty issue one encounters in ethical theory. Here too a concept audit of the proprieties of careful discussion can not only clarify the issues but bring some of its instructive features into clearer light.

A delegation of function differs from mere substitution or replacement. Substitution is binary: one party functions in place of another as it replacement. Delegation is in fact triadic: One delegate something to someone: B functions as A's delegate and by his (A's) authorization in a certain range of matters (R). The delegate acts FOR and not just IN PLACE OF another within a certain sphere of action. In mock-warfare the king delegates his champion to fight in his (the king's) place and on his behalf. And when his proxy prevails this counts as a victory in the king's cause.

Delegation is transitory. Unlike the person who resigns a role in favor of a predesigned successor, the delegator fully retains all of the functions—rights and obligations alike—of the role encompassed in the delegation. Again, suppose a teacher of small children has a medical problem. If she enlists someone to fill in for her, she delegates. However, if the principal arranges for someone to substitute for her, there is no delegation. It is a matter of who bears responsibility for the proxy that is arranged for: with the agent herself there is delegation; with a duly-empowered third party there is no delegation.

Delegation occurs responsibly or irresponsibly according to the delegator's well-grounded expectations about the delegatee's competence in relevant regards. And especially when the interests of others—even third parties—are involved the delegate will bear such responsibility in the matter.

The vacationing physician who commits his patients into the hands of a replacing locum bears responsibility for this doctor's competent performance.

In many contexts delegation is a normal and established practice. In hierarchical organizations superiors standardly delegate some of their functions and powers and responsibilities to others. But in matters of performance where the crux is one of the talent and skill rather than status and entitlement, delegation is not at issue. When I ask you to play for me in a tennis game or bridge game, you are not functioning as my delegate.

In this context the difference between a proxy and a substitute is crucial: the substitute merely replaces whereas the proxy represents as a delegate. When you act as my proxy, I am still figuratively present and you act on my behalf; when you are my replacement I am absent from the scene and remain inactive and uninvolved. An actor's understudy is her substitute but not her delegate. And the same holds with a proxy wedding.

SOME LIMITS OF DELEGATION

In principle, many of the things we do in life can be delegated to others—often with considerable advantage. But many cannot. You can convey my apology, but you cannot apologize for me. And the same holds for vouching for someone. These are things I cannot delegate because my personal involvement is of the essence.

Accordingly, stage performance cannot be delegated. The understudy does indeed act the role but does not do so as delegate of the replaced actor. Nor can you properly woo for another—think here of Cyrano de Bergerac or of John Alden. Filling in for an unavailable actor is not delegation. Moreover, creativity cannot be delegated: the "of the school of" painter is not a proper proxy.

And turning to matters of knowledge and belief, I can certainly delegate to someone else the resolution of what is to be the content of my beliefs, but theirs is only the decision what to recommend, the decision to accept still remains mine. I alone can do my believing. The dream to adopt your view of the matter and confirm the substance of my believing to yours is my decision. Belief formation must be done on one's own account: it is non-delegable. Even when I accept your judgments, and yield your authority, the commitment remains mine.

Now on to decision.

Determining the outcome of decision is something I can delegate to another—and perhaps even to a machine (as per a coin toss). But while delegate to you the resolution of a decision issue. But accepting the result—and thereby actually *making that decision*—is something I cannot delegate. My decision will have to remain my own and I will retain the responsibility.

A delegated decision still counts as a decision of the delegating agent. And this is the case with ultimate responsibility in general. When my proxy acts for me, it is still for me—in my name and on my account—that he acts. Alike in matters of belief and decision alike ultimately responsibility is unalienable.

And this holds for matters of action as well. When I hire a hit man to commit my murder for me I am still a murderer and not only in the eye of the law but also in the eyes of a moralist.

There are, moreover, many kinds of actions I cannot delegate, things for which I have executive responsibility by their very nature.

Commissioning someone to be one's charity dispenser, still leaves the original donor as the benefactor. Decisions regarding the recipients can be delegated. But the actual giving cannot. Charity as such is inalienable.

Or consider another case. I am to be get-away driver for the heist. Flu knocks me out at the last moment and I recruit a buddy to be my substitute. But he is now not my proxy but my replacement. I conspire, yes; but I do not rob: robbery participation is undelegable.

Any performance in which affection is needed cannot be delegated. You can act as my proxy in a marriage ceremony but not in a marriage.

From the moral point of view it is a salient fact that delegation does not abrogate responsibility; does not transfer responsibility (or capability) from the delegator to the delegatee. This delegates must be chosen with care and with attention to their conscientiousness. For only where the delegate "clearly acts beyond his instructions" is he responsible in this own right.

A CURIOUS DISPARITY

In ethical regards, then, delegation involves a curious asymmetry. When *A* delegates to *B* the exercise of certain functions that relate to *C*'s interests then *A* continues to bear responsibility. Thus, if Jones undertakes to manage some of Smith's funds and turns over to Robinson who mishandles them, Jones continues to bear full responsibility notwithstanding the delegation: the responsibility is unalienable. But if Robinson performs unconsciously and unforeseeably well, then Jones must cede or at least share the credit. (There is an asymmetry between blame and credit here.)

But be this as it may, the fact remains that delegation is a complex concept with intricate ethical involvements. A concept audit here brings to light a fertile manifold of issues demanding due heed in the deliberations of moral philosophy.

#32

Doing Unto Others

It is often maintained that morality requires us to treat others as one would treat oneself. But it appears that there we must admit exceptions to this rule because there will be a significant difference in point of respect.

Consider the following situation.

Let it be that one can purchase a certain lottery ticket at a price of $1.00 and that one can do so for oneself or for another. But the owner of the ticket has a one in ten thousand chance of winning a million dollars and a one in a million chance of incurring a penalty of a million dollars.

The expected value of the ticket is $99, and since you can buy it for a dollar, it looks to be a good bet to buy it for oneself. But in doing so one accepts the risk of a catastrophic loss, which is something you might well be willing to take in stride given the favorable outlook of the situation. So if the person for whom you are buying the ticket is yourself, you may well say "This is a good gamble, and I'll accept its risk, so I'll buy this lottery ticket for myself."

However, if the person who is to own the ticket is someone else, you may well reason: "I really must not buy this ticket for X. For in doing so I am creating a situation where he incurs the risk of possible catastrophe."

There is an instructive lesson here. We are morally free to take risks on our own behalf, but not on behalf of others. When undiluted positivities are at issue, we should doubtless treat others as we would ourselves. But when negativities are also in the picture, the idea of putting others to a risk one might well take in stride for oneself is no longer appropriate.

And so, significant conceptual lesson emerges here: the character of the stakes at issue with one's actions will make a morally significant difference in regard to doing to others as one would so for oneself.

#33

Faux Quantities

QUALITY PROBLEMS

Social and political philosophers often speak of such quantities as the "age of consent" for sexual engagement, the "age of adulthood" for criminal liability, the "age of eligibility" for voting, or for the "age of maturity" for entering into legal contracts or into military service.

All this sort of thing is of course based upon a palpable fiction. The day before age X one is unsuited and ineligible, on the day itself one is fully qualified. And of course reality is nothing like that. Neither for individuals nor groups is there a clear cut-off quantity of this sort: a day earlier unfitted and ineligible, a day later fully ready and able. Nature just does not work like that with clear breaks and surgically neat meet boundaries. Individuals move by slow stages and indeed by advances and regressions: And different individuals do so with different periodization and at different paces.

And this all too obvious fact has some significant implications.

QUANTITY ILLUSIONS

First off, it means that this entire idea of quantity of transition threshold has no legitimate place at all in social theory and political philosophy. These "quantities" are nonquantities and the entire issue is a pretense, a mere fiction that bears as little relation to reality as does the rule that a person missing for seven years is dead.

And second, it means that these faux quantities are no more than fictional contrivances to which sometimes resort for the sake of simplicity, uniformity, and convenience in the management of society's affairs. . . . substantially arbitrary, fact ignoring contrivance to facilitate the transaction of public business.

A pseudo-quantity like the "age of consent" does not *find* a difference between what is too little and too great, but *makes* it. In advance of their postulation there is nothing measurable for such quantification to fix upon.

Political and social theorist have no business concerning themselves with such merely practical contrivances. They are as much a social fact as is the "rule of the road" that provides for right- (or left-) sided traffic.

To treat these faux quantities as genuine *quantities* is to commit the error of making them into genuine social parameters such as life expectancy or suicide rates. Social convention apart they lack a factual basis. Within a range of alternatives their specific rationale is utilitarian rather than descriptive. A concept audit of the issues shows that treating such items as objectively defined quantities would be to commit a category mistake.

Luck versus Fortune

A KEY DISTINCTION

Attention to conscientious usage reflects a significant distinction between luck and fortune—one that is often neglected in philosophical discussions of the relevant issues.

To be lucky you have to do something: luck (be it good or bad) is a response to agency that lies outside the range of effective foreseeability on your part. You are lucky if you win the lottery, find a treasure trove, leave the building just before a gas explosion, or work for an understanding employer. By contrast when something good or bad happens to you without active interaction on your part, then you are fortunate or the reverse—irrespective of whether or not this outcome was foreseeable. You are fortunate to have a healthy constitution, to have been born to affluent parents, to live in a time when dentistry is painless. But all of these are things you did nothing about. Even if the house you have just moved into is destroyed by an earthquake, you are rather unfortunate than unlucky. Often there are overlaps. If your spouse unexpectedly comes into a large inheritance you can consider yourself both fortunate and lucky.

Both luck and fortune are matters that lie outside our control—we deserve neither credit nor blame for the things they bring our way.

One is not responsible for good or ill fortune, and gets no credit or blame for it. By contrast, luck can be a matter of ill- or well-advised exposure. It can, in principle, work to the credit or discredit of its possessor.

There is thus a significant difference between luck and fortune. You are fortunate if something good happens to or for you in the natural course of things. But you are lucky when such a benefit results from something that you do and does so despite its being chancy—and particularly so if it occurs against the odds and reasonable expectations. A person who has inherited enough money to be able to travel first class is fortunate but not strictly speaking lucky. And so is the airline passenger who finds himself shifted from coach to first class for the convenience of the airline. Fate and fortune relate to the conditions and circumstances of our lives generally, luck to the episodic goods and evils that chance to befall us in consequence of our choices.[1] Our innate skills and talents are matters of good fortune; the opportunities that chance brings our way to help us develop them are for the most part matters of good luck. Contracting a cold is merely unfortunate, seeing that it is something that people do pretty regularly, and which can therefore be foreseen in general terms; but its happening on the evening chosen for one's opening night performance is distinctly unlucky.

The positive and negative things that come one's way in the world's ordinary course—including one's heritage (biological, medical, social, economic), one's abilities and talents, the circumstances of one's place and time (be they peaceful or chaotic, for example)—all these are matters of what might be characterized as fate and fortune. People are not unlucky to be born timid or ill-tempered, just unfortunate. But the positivities and negativities that come one's way by chance and unforeseen happenstance—finding a treasure trove, for example, or walking away from an accident fatal to most others—are matters of luck. It was (modestly) fortunate for John Doe that he owned a pen-knife. But it was distinctly lucky for him that he happened to have it along on the day he needed it to deal with a snake bite. (He didn't generally carry the knife, but just by chance took it with him on that particular day.) You are heir to a great estate by auspicious fortune, but you are lucky when you inherit it just in the nick of time to save you from bankruptcy. Luck and chance are two sides of the same coin. But fate is something else again, something from which the element of chance is missing.

Suppose that we discover that a large but heretofore undetected meteor is on a collision course with the earth. Humanity's fate is sealed, the handwriting is on the wall. By a fixed number of days hence, the earth will be covered by a thick cloud of debris and will become unable to sustain mammalian life. What a catastrophe! In these circumstances, however, our extinction would (strictly speaking) be unfortunate rather than unlucky. It is just the element of surprise—of chanciness and impredictability—that distinguishes luck from fate or fortune at large.[2]

Luck is to some extent manipulatable—not because one can bring chance under control, but because one can put oneself in the way of its doing some good (or harm!). The key point is that to have luck you must *do* something: if you do not buy a ticket, you cannot win the lottery. Whether or not you *can* have luck hinges on your actions. With luck, as with much else in life, when opportunity knocks one has to open the door. But of course whether or not luck will favor you when you open the way is something entirely beyond your control.

The chanciness of luck means that in interactions where one party runs all the risks only one can be lucky. The sponsors of a lottery are destined for gain—here only the players can be lucky. And the same holds for gambling casinos where things are managed in such a way that the house "takes no chances."

And so while we can (in certain circumstances) be *fortunate* to be red-headed (say when this makes one eligible for some benefit or other), one cannot be *lucky* to be a red-head. One can, however, be lucky in that it was red-headed individuals whom the institutor of the benefit at issue just happened to fix upon as the beneficiaries of her largesse. Luck as such must be chancy. And this is reflected in luck's volatility and inconsistency. A Scottish proverb, cited as early as 1721, says "Behind bad luck comes good luck." (The reverse would be just as true!) And another old proverb insists that "The only sure thing about luck is that it will change."

SOME IMPLICATIONS

Only if one takes too literally the idea of a *lot* in life—by (quite absurdly) thinking of human biographies in terms of a lottery of life-plan allocations to *preexistingly* identifiable individuals—can one conceptualize a person's overall fate or destiny in terms of luck. For only then would the sum total of all the goods and evils befalling people become reduced—comprehensively and automatically— to a matter of chance allocation. This is obviously unrealistic. Accordingly, a person can be fortunate to have a good disposition or a talent for mathematics, but she cannot be *lucky* in these regards because chance is not involved. Her disposition and talents are part of what makes someone the individual she is; it is not something that chance happens to bring along and superadd to a preexisting identity. One can indeed be lucky to encounter a person who induces or helps one to develop a talent. But having that talent itself is a matter of fortune rather than good luck. It makes no sense to assimilate personal fate to games of chance because with games there is always antecedently a player to enter into participation, while with people there is no antecedent, identity-bereft individual who draws the lot at issue with a particular endowment.

To be sure, the distinction at issue is a matter rather of the properties that of the invariable actualities of usage. A certain degree of verbal legislation is involved. When we ask the girl who tells us that she has just become engaged "and who's the lucky man?" we should, on present telling, strictly speaking have to say "*fortunate* man" if we wish to avoid any limit of suggestion that he picked her name out of a hat. The distinction here drawn between luck and fortune on the basis of the chanciness of the former is honored in common usage by the occasional breach.

In this context a concept audit is useful and productive. For, in neglecting the distinction between luck and fortune, theorists fail to do justice to a significant feature in the philosophy of life. A concept audit of the ideas at work in the terminology-range of luck, fortune, chance, fortuitous occurrence, and their cognates provides instructive insights into the nature of the human condition.

NOTES

1. The luck/fate distinction goes back to classical antiquity. For the ancients, distinguished between haphazard *fortuna* (which operates by accident and chance) and necessitarian *fatum* (which operates according to fixed deterministic laws).

2. A word about impredictability/unpredictability is in order here. A phenomenon is unpredictable when it is erratic: when it varies eccentrically in ways which can perfectly well be foreseen—at least in general terms. A phenomenon is impredictable when it eludes any and all possibility of rationally based foresight.

The Problem of Progress

THE IDEA OF PROGRESS

Philosophers have been caught up in a seemingly endless debate over the question of whether mankind is making progress in one area or another of philosophical concern: morality, culture, are, and even philosophy itself, etc. But here much of the problem roots in the very idea of progress. For close attention to the concepts of progress, advance, betterment, and their cognates show that two distinct albeit related matters can be at issue.

When one is moving toward a definite destination then every step forward from one's start is a step closer to this goal. So when you are counting from 1 to 1,000, each count-step carries you one step forward to completing the project, and you make progress correspondingly. Here, steps forward afford a perfectly plausible measures of progress.

But suppose your project is to count off the prime numbers—all of them *in toto*. Then no matter how far along you are there yet remains just as many steps to go as you confronted at the outset. You are getting no nearer to your destination: you advance, but do not progress. With such a project that lacks a definite end such "progress" as one makes in moving onward brings one no closer to the destination one has in view.

SOME PROBLEMATIC CASES

Suppose your aim is to master arithmetic. Each time you learn to avoid a certain mistake your performance improves. But you are making no progress toward your (actually unreachable) goal. The road to arithmetical mastery is not constructed by error evidence. No matter how many sorts of errors you eliminate an infinitude of others possibilities remain. In any domain where the possibilities of error are unending, one faces the paradox of ongoing elimination without achievable eradication.

To be sure in all such cases one improves matters by doing. One can increase the range of cases where things go right without reducing the range of cases where things can go wrong. But in these cases the essential core of progress—reducing the scope of what yet remains to be done—cannot be achieved. One makes headway but no real progress. One is embarked on a labor of Sisyphus, and this is the very paradigm of a situation where making progress is impossible.

In the absence of a definite and realizable goal, "progress" as assessed in terms of motion forward is not real progress at all if this calls for making headway toward goal achievement. Only where a definite and achievable destination is in view—where moving away from the start is correlative with coming closer to the end—is the idea of progress unproblematically applicable. It would accordingly be a mistake to identify progress with mere improvement, and one would do well to distinguish between moving increasingly from an initial point of departure and drawing closer to a desired destination, with only the latter unproblematically constituting genuine progress.

As a matter of principle such projects as mastering the facts of a topic let alone achieving moral perfection do not admit of making progress in the root sense of goal approximation. For where there is no fixed destination we cannot possibly make progress toward its realization. An instructive and oft-overlooked conclusion emerges here: improvement is not correlative with progress.

And this bears instructively upon the issues of our initial paragraph. Of course, we can make *improvements* in the levels of moral comportment, cultural achievement, artistic productivity, philosophical understanding, etc. But real progress is something which is in principle impracticable in these fields—not because of an impossibility of doing more or doing better, but because what is at issue with coming closer to goal realization is something which concept-auditing shows to be unrealizable.

#36

Issues of Excellence

WHAT IS EXCELLENCE?

A not infrequent result of concept auditing is finding that something that looks simple at first view actually is far from it. Take the idea of excellence. Seemingly it simply means "of the highest quality." But that is only the beginning of a long and convoluted story.

Granted, to be excellent is to excel. But excelling is always a matter of respect: for one item to excel another is to have this condition in this or that particular respect, that is, to achieve a qualitative superiority in one or another specific regard. There are, accordingly, many different ways of excelling and excellence can be achieved in many different modes:

- power ("your excellency")
- wealth ("rich as Croesus")
- performance (in music, sports, mathematics, etc.)
- social standing ("the top 100")
- workmanship ("a masterpiece")
- beauty ("Mirror, mirror, on the wall")
- etc.

Excellence, like quality assessment in general, always envisions a limited comparison range denominated by a duly subordinated taxonomic category. There is no such thing as an excellent item or an excellent action; unlike the situation of an excellent hammer or an excellent musical performance. An item cannot just be excellent: it has to be an excellent *something*. Excellence cannot be detached from taxonomy. The only meaningful sort of excellence is that bound up with the proviso: of its kind. And this taxonomic aspect of excellence means that the conception can proliferate aspectivally. There is no such thing as an excellent dog as such, but only an excellent show dog or hunting dog or guard dog, etc. The things characterized as excellent will be so *sui generis*. Accordingly, excellence is a highly syncategorematic concept: it cuts across the usual boundaries and comes into operation across a virtually endless range of different sorts of things. And there is effectively nothing in the way of descriptive properties that different kinds of excellent things—an excellent mathematical proofs, for example, and an excellent dachshund— need to have in common.

However, a dog cannot be excellent in a species-indifferent, all-purpose way. It can be an excellent sheepdog, or excellent hunter, or excellent guide dog, etc. Different capacities and capabilities are at issue and they need not and will be comaximizable. Again, to be economical to operate a house must be small; to be open, spacious it must be large. To be convenient for work, shopping, entertainment it must be in town; to be quiet, private, scenically positioned it must be in the country. Different desiderata and often not conjointly realizable. Choices will have to be made not just on grounds of economy but on grounds of feasibility. The parameters of merit reflective of different value dimensions and distinct desiderata are not in general comaximizable. They will have to be balanced in a way that demands a shift from maximization to optimization. And in most contexts this calls for introducing considerations of aims, purposes, and use—for viewing matters in a pragmatic light.

Excellence is an evaluative rather than descriptive feature. And it can be exhibited across a wider or narrower range. One can be an excellent athlete or an excellent linguist, and there can be excellent roses and excellent hammers. To be sure, there are realms in which there is no room or place for quality assessment. Numbers, for example—one integer is not better (or worse) than another. Accordingly there simply are no excellent integers—one can be larger than another, but not better than it. Of course, this does not mean that there is no quality assessment in mathematics at all. This would assuredly be false, for clearly one proof of the thesis can be more elegant, direct, economical, accessible than another. There are no excellent integers, but there are certainly excellent proofs.

And yet another consideration comes to the fore here, namely that there are two rather different sorts of qualitative comparisons. On the one hand there is a comparison between types (as when one compares beagles vs. dachshunds in their capacity for serving as hunting dogs) and on the other hand there is a comparison between individuals (as when one compares two particular beagles in this regard). One must thus differentiate between the merit assessment of thing-kinds ("apples vs. oranges" or one kind of apple vs. another) and instance assessments (the overall quality of one Granny Smith apple in comparison to another). There are both kind-comparative evaluations and instance-comparative evaluations, and excellence assessment can proceed by different criteriological evaluation standards. As the three goddesses taught Paris, judging excellence can be a tricky business.

THE CRITERIOLOGY OF EXCELLENCE: DIMENSIONS OF MERIT

Many kinds of things have a particular group of positive features characteristic of that type of thing. (e.g., with automobiles we have: reliability, drivability, operating economy, ride comfort, etc.). These positive features define a *mode of excellence* for that particular type of thing. And those type-members that exhibit these modes of excellence in virtually all relevant regards constitute the quality-elite for this thing-type. And whether it is pick-up trucks or maternity hospitals, McIntosh apples or tourist hotels, every sort of thing that has a use or function will admit of a quality elite that commands special consideration.

Often there are clear-cut criteria by which modes of excellence can be assessed. Thus in recent years it has been a common practice in the United States to rate cities in point of "livability," this being measured by such factors as Art Resources, Climate, Crime, Economy, Education, Healthcare, Housing, Recreation, and Transportation.

With wines (of a given type and region) there are such factors as: pleasant taste, complexity, aroma/bouquet, transparency, color, and alcohol content. And obviously these qualitative parameters will differ markedly with different types of things. In different contexts excellence calls for a very diversified and highly contextualized variety of factors. An excellent coffee has to taste quite differently from an excellent tea: very different excellence-making features are at issue. (Note that an excellence determinative feature in one context may even be in conflict with that of another. Massive weight is an asset for pigs but a detriment for humans.)

Category-relative assessment will call for very difference criteria. With one species of dog whiskers will count far more than tails, with another the reverse may hold. Cleanliness and service are key quality factors with all restaurants, but with neighborhood diner presentation and creativity take a back seat to speed and courteous service, while with purgoers of haute cuisine the reverse is likely the case.

Various types of things have *merit-determinative features* and it would be instructive to have an explicit register constituting a checklist of excellence-indicative factors in various contexts: These provide for a checklist of aspect of quality along the following lines:

- *fine art paintings*: producer-eminence, "importance," thematic significance, traceable provenance, condition
- *automobiles*: performance, reliability, operating economy, ride comfort, seating comfort, crash safety, condition
- *beauty-pageant contestants*: poise, "charm," figure ("swim suit"), talent, articulation
- *show dogs* (highly variable criteria by breed)
- *college professors*: performance as teachers, scholars, colleagues, administrators
- *hotels* (stars allotted by quality of rooms, furnishings, service, etc.)
- *restaurants* (stars allocated by food quality, presentation, service, atmosphere, hygiene)
- *dancing or figure skating performances* (varied and complex criteria)
- *wines* ("bouquet," taste, color, alcohol content, etc.)
- *status of personal health* (weight, BMI, blood pressure, pulse, etc.)
- *farm animals* (species-variable criteria as used in awards at agricultural fairs, e.g., for pigs, cows, sheep, etc.)

Different versions of excellence manifest themselves in different ways. Performatively a clear observer is a better news reporter; functionally an unbroken window a better window; and ontologically, an intelligible poem is thereby a better poem.

All the same, the idea of excellence in this or that respect could not be implemented, and the evolution of excellence could not proceed, in the absence of appropriate criteriological standards. To be sure, it is often effectively impossible to spell out explicitly *all* of the standards for the determination of excellence: with poems or films, for example, or paintings. Achieving totality in regard to the requisites of excellence is generally impracticable: there are sometimes just too many ways in which things can go wrong.

Sometimes the situation grows so complex that only the informal judgment of experience experts can integrate the multiplicity of factors involved.

Whenever excellence has to be adjusted by informal estimation rather than objectivity determinable criterion it is obviously preferable to trust the views of experts. Telling substantiation for this is afforded by such competitive contests as ice skating or ballroom dancing. To the untutored eye it all looks to be superbly done. Only the trained eye is alert to the finer points and nuances of performance that distinguish between the highly competent and the truly excellent.

But why should it be that those certain features are excellence-indicative for a particular type of thing? How is one to account for their type-positivity? As foreshadowed above, three sorts of reasons are basically at issue here.

1. *Functional reasons*: a certain sort of aim or function is at issue with this type of thing, and the possession of these features enable its possessor better to fulfill its function.
2. *Performatory reasons*: a certain sort of performance or process is at issue with this type of thing, and the possession of these features enables its possessor to carry these out more efficiently, effectively, and elegantly.
3. *Ontological reasons*: possession of those features serves to qualify their possessors as a better (clearer, more representative, or more typical) instance or example of the type of thing that it is.

Among these factors, functional efficacy is particularly important. Thus given the sort of function that automobiles serve, and taking account of the condition and circumstances under which they must serve this function, it is clear that operating economy is indispensable here. Nowhere is the functionality of qualitative criteria more evident than in the increasingly popular ratings of cities in point of livability. For the salient criteria will have to differ greatly on whether those at issue are to be twenty-somethings or senior citizens, athletes or high-school valedictorians, blue-collar workers or academics. As such examples convincingly illustrate, criteria themselves afford functional resources that are appropriate, as such, to the extent that they serve effectively and purposes for which quality assessment is at stake.

FACTOR INTEGRATION PROBLEMS

In setting the desiderata that constitute the determinative factors of merit it is relatively easy to specify the *necessary, sine qua non* conditions. But *sufficient* conditions are something else again. It must be acknowledged that it is often a matter of considerable theoretical difficulty to combine the *aspectival* quality assessments into one single over-all evaluation. For even when the totality of the discernibly necessary conditions is conjoined, their sufficiency will generally still be problematic, seeing that even when all of those specified desiderata are there, the possibility of an unforeseen spoiler cannot in general be eliminated. Explicit criteriology may then require informal judgment.

There is a daunting problem in integrating subordinate modes of merit into one synoptic overall result. For example, we might contemplate a situation of four parameters of merit (A, B, C, D) with each desideratum potentially realized to an extent characterized as H (high), M (middling), and L (low). And we shall envision a situation where excellence is achieved is subject to the following conditions

QUALIFYING CONDITIONS FOR EXCELLENCE

Desideratum		Level of realization (for qualifying as excellent)
A	H	H
B	H	M
C	X	H
D	X	H

Note: X can be either *H* or *M*.

Figure 36.1

No value parameter can be *L*. *A* must be *H*. And if *B* is also *H* then *C* and *D* no longer matter. But if *B* is not also *H*, then both *C* and *D* must be *H*.

As Figure 36.1 indicates, there will thus be five combinational modes in which excellence is achieved. There is, however, no numeral formula of combination that can achieve an appropriate resolution for this complex situation.[1]

One salient reason for this is the phenomenon of what might be called *desideratum discord* where in advancing with one positivity we automatically diminish another. What we have here is vividly manifested in the phenomenon of *positivity complementarity* that obtains when two parameters of merit are so interconnected that more of one automatically means less of the other, as per Figure 36.2.

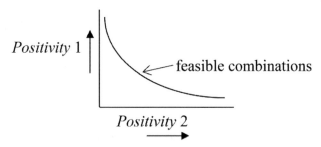

Figure 36.2

The crux here is that one aspect of merit can be augmented only at the price of diminishing another.

We shall characterize as a Teeter-Totter Condition any arrangement where an improvement in regard to one aspect can only be achieved at the cost of worsening matters in another respect. And whenever two inherently positive factors are (like familiarity and novelty) locked into such a teeter-totter relationship we cannot have it both ways.

QUALITY AND QUANTITY: EXCELLENCE AND ELITES

As Spinoza observed, excellent things are difficult and rare. To be excellent is to excel, that is to stand above the crowd—to be substantially superior in whatever respect may be at issue to the great mass of otherwise kindred items. To be an excellent X is generally to be better at being an X than the vast majority of other X's. But just exactly how much better? The short, rough-and-ready answer is better than some large percentage of them. Quality has a quantitative side, seeing that, as Spinoza has it at the end of his *Ethics*, all excellent things are as difficult as they are rare.[2] It lies in the nature of things that as we "raise the bar" on qualitative superiority the pool of qualified prospects shrinks to ever-smaller proportions.

There is in general an inverse correlation between the magnitude of achievement and the number of achievers. In particular consider the four sorts of situations represented by the curves of Figure 36.3. Observe that excellence becomes increasingly difficult as we move from type (A) to type (D). In general, as the quality-level as issue decreases (i.e., declines from first-rate to fifth-rate) the number of items at or above that quality level will increase markedly.[3]

Consider type (D) in particular. Here one would have a distribution that attributes a small percentage (say 5%) to level 1, a large percentage (say 65%) to level 5, with a more or less equal percentage distribution across the three intermediate levels (say roughly 12% each). For example, with ranks in the U.S. military we have[4]:

1. Senior Officers (General and field rank) 3%
2. Junior Officers (Company-grade officers) 13%
3. Senior NCOs (Grades E7–E9) 10%
4. Mid-level NCOs (Grade E6) 12%
5. Enlisted and Junior NCOs (Grade E1–E5) 61%

This clearly approximates to a type (D) distribution. However, while excellence is in general rare, rarity alone does not necessarily make for excellence. The quality distribution will be contingently dependent on the nature of the factor at issue. There are sometimes just as many inferior Xs as superior ones. But this is exceptional and not the rule. Often the quality at a given level is proportional not to quantity of the total number of items involved, but merely to its logarithm. (This has the consequence that the total number of items must increase exponentially over time to maintain a merely linear increase in high quality items, a phenomenon exhibited in the fruits of scientific research.[5])

It is instructive in this regard to consider the idea of cognitive excellence in relation to the importance of ideas: the two go pretty much hand in hand. In the setting of a (hypothetical) ideal treatise we might say that (1) there are roughly on average 10 chapters per book, 10 sections per chapter, 10 paragraphs per section, 10 sentences per paragraph, and 10 words per sentence. So if the amount of text allocated to a given idea reflects its importance then we will have in the contrast of our hypothetically idealized treatise:

10^1 = 10 ideas of (at least) the first importance (level I): excellence
10^2 = 100 ideas of (at least) the second importance (level II): superiority
10^3 = 1000 ideas of (at least) the third importance (level III): worthiness

And so on. With each quality level separated from the next by the factor of 10, we have an overall quantity quality distribution along the lines of the exponential growth pattern (D) of Figure 36.3.

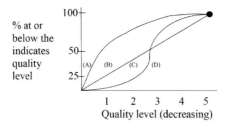

NOTE: The diagram contemplates five quality-rating levels:

  excellent > superior > good > mediocre > inferior

There are basically four prospects for a quality/quantity relation: (A) convex, (2) linear, (C) S-shaped, and (D) concave. They represent distributively different modes of quality/quantity interrelation with increasing elitism as we move from (A) to (D). With (D) we have to note the uncommon phenomenon that numbers increase exponentially when the level of quality declines.

Figure 36.3

Sometimes excellence does not look to be all that rare. The students in an algebra class can all be excellent (should the teacher happen to be very lucky) and deserving of an A-plus. But here as ever the comparison group is the crucial factor for excellence. For the contemplated situation to obtain those students must be substantially better not than their classmates but the algebra students at large. (Otherwise there is simply "grade-inflation.") A properly constructed comparison class is crucial for the assessment of excellence. To be sure, in theory it is possible for the majority of a group to manage doing some performance extremely well. Everyone in a certain village may be a

SCIENTIFIC PRODUCTIVITY

(in terms of publication in major professional journals)

Top % of producers	Aggregate proportion of their production
2%	25%
10%	40%
25%	55%
75%	75%
100%	100%

Note 1: Data of this type conforms to what is known as "Lotka's Law." For details see D. J. DeSolla Price, *Big Science, Little Science* (NY: Columbia University Press, 1963).
Note 2: The five productivity groups of producers may be designated as grades 1–5, respectively. The aggregate total productivity within these five quality grades will then be 25%, 15%, 15%, 20%, and 25%, respectively. In terms of the Figure 36.3 categories we have something of a type (B) distribution.

Figure 36.4

ment of affairs, the allocation of effort, competitions, prizes and awards, remuneration. In general, excellence is not its own reward but receives "recognition" in some external way—if only in terms of respect. But in actual practice, performatory excellence is generally rewarded, but the extent to which this transpires depends critically on the Law of Supply and Demand. Anesthesiologists outearn dermatologists, educational administrators are paid more than classroom teachers. No doubt excellence has its financial advantage in most every field, but quality ranking is only occasionally a prime determinant of earning power.

EXCELLENCE IN PRAGMATIC PERSPECTIVE

One must acknowledge that in theory a quality landscape can (in theory) be flat with all individuals being of roughly the same quality thus constituting a quality democracy, as it were, where one thing is every bit as good as another. (e.g., the criminal law should envision no elite: everyone should stand before it on the same level.) But in such a sphere the concept of excellence simply has no place. It is, by nature, designed to achieve discrimination with a view to some sort of implementation—even if only in judgment and attitude. In most contexts natural and artificial alike quality assessment is intended to yield differential results and the positive outliers of excellence are very much in prospect.

Its functional role as a category of evaluative assessment endows the ideas of excellence an ineradicably pragmatic aspect. After all, evaluation as a rational procedure is not an exercise in abstract ratiocination—is by its very notion a telic and purposive activity—it is always with some end in view. And, as noted above, three sorts of considerations that are operative here, namely performatory reasons, functional reasons, and classificatory reasons. And all three operate with a view to ends, objectives, and purposes. (A mere taxonomy will have a purpose even when the items that it classifies do not.) Evaluative assessment always has some end or purpose in view: a hammer is excellent (or not) for use in nailing; a beagle is excellent (or not) for use in tracking; a man is excellent (or not) as a mathematician or a sprinter or a family-provider.

To evaluate is to acknowledge that there must be a difference in point of what to do about it for if this were not the case, quality assessment would be pointless. The conception of excellence affords a decision-making tool. By its means we identify its bearers with an end in view: we seek excellence because we wish to achieve, cultivate, acknowledge, and promote those things that deserve its accolade.

As a careful audit of the concept show, in the end, excellence is not so much a theoretical as a practical virtue.

NOTES

1. The complexity resides in the fact that as long as both *A* and *B* are *H*, any of the others can be as low as *M*; but *B* can also be *M* as long as *C* and *D* are *H*. No assignment of weights will achieve this result in a blending process.
2. Spinoza, Ethics, bk., v., prop. 41, Scholium, ad fin.
3. For details regarding this phenomenon, see Zipf, 1949.
4. Source: Statistical Abstracts of the United States.
5. For details see Rescher, 1969.
6. Source: Statistical Abstract of the United States.

REFERENCES

Derek J. Price. *Little Science, Big Science* (New York: Columbia University Press, 1963).
Nicholas Rescher, *Introduction to Value Theory* (Engelwood Cliffs: Prentice Hall, 1969).

Nicholas Rescher, *Scientific Progress* (Oxford: Blackwell, 1978). *Statistical Abstracts of the United States* (2011–2012).

J. O. Urmson, "On Grading," *Mind*, vol. 59, (1950), pp. 145–169.

George K. Zipf, *Human Behavior and the Principle of Least Effort* (Cambridge, Mass., Addison-Wesley Press, 1949).

#37

Problems of Perfection

MERIT CONFLICTS EXCLUDE ABSOLUTE PERFECTION

Aristotle had it that perfection (*teleion*) is "that which in respect of excellence and merit cannot be excellent on its kind, ... lacking nothing in respect of the form of their proper excellence."[1] And as commonly conceived of by philosophers, perfection is a matter of excellence in every relevant respect, achieving the utmost throughout the range of relevant positivity.

However, a concept audit of this idea brings to light a problematic element of inherent unrealism.

The reality of it is that any object of evaluative appraisal is going to have a plurality of modes of merit—various different sorts of possible virtues and defects. And these parameters of merit can interact. They can be concordant (mutually reinforcing) or discordant (mutually supplementary).

For example, conflict exists in situations of that central case whenever two factors are so related that one of them can only be increased at the cost of diminishing the other. One may want a residence to be both spacious and easily maintained, but the one is clearly at odds with the other, with more here demanding less there. Such *merit complementarity* arises whenever two desiderata are at odds with one another. Such discord is clearly a common, nay virtually universal phenomena. Both spaciousness and economy of maintenance are virtues of a domestic residence, but there is an inherent conflict between them because greater extent requires more extensive cleaning. Both ample legroom and maneuverability are virtues of automobiles but longer cars require more turning room. On the other hand, merits are mutually convenient when they reinforce one another, as would be the case with the crash safety of an automobile and its riding comfort, both of which are brought up with the car's overall weight.

Such relationships can be illustrated by a 3 × 3 interrelation diagram (Figures 37.1 and 37.2) where two types of merit can be realized to an extent that is high (H) or medium (M) or low (L):

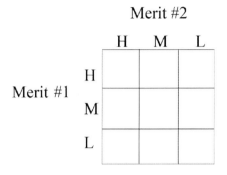

Figure 37.1

Each of these nine compartments can be indicated as either feasible (√) or infeasible (X) in the evaluative context at issue. Accordingly, the three conditions referred to above will correspond to Figure 37.2.

CONCORDANCE

	H	M	L
H	√	X	X
M	X	√	X
L	X	X	√

CONFLICT

	H	M	L
H	X	√	√
M	X	√	X
L	√	X	X

INDEPENDENCE

	H	M	L
H	√	√	√
M	√	√	√
L	√	√	√

Figure 37.2

Every relevant object of evaluation is bound to exhibit a combination of aspects of merit and demerit related in one of these ways.

MODES OF PERFECTION

For present purposes, however, the issue of merit complementarity has particular importance. For in situations of multi-factor validation, where some of these factors stand in conflict or competition with others, not every parameter of merit can be increased at one and the same time. With all cases of this sort it is inevitable that that *perfection*—that is, the concurrent maximization of every mode of merit—is simply impossible.

The idea of perfection is therefore going to have to be regarded from a different angle and viewed in a different light. Fortunately there is a promising prospect here. For in theory there are two different ways of looking at perfections:

i.   *The route of positivity* (*via positiva*): We begin by surveying the relevant modes of merit, of positivity. And we require concurrent maximal positivity in respect to all of these.
ii. *The route of negativity* (*via negativa*): We begin by surveying all the relative modes of demerit, the type of flaw, or negativity. And we require concurrent maximal negativity, that is, total absence—in respect to all of them.

Perfection in this second construction is simply flawlessness—the absence of outright defects. And this is a very real prospect even in cases of merit complementarity.

A concept audit of the idea of perfection thus leads to the conclusion that if one expects to have a concept that can actually do real work—that can, in principle, have a realizable range of applicability, then one must distinguish between a positive and a negative approach to the matter—and adopt the latter. The classic conception of unconfirmed excellence is simply unrealistic—not because it asks for so much in practice but because it asks for what is impossible *in principle*.

And such a concept audit has an instructive bearing on the previous chapter's theme of progress. For they clearly indicate that this idea makes unproblematic sense only in the negative and not in the positive mode. The achievement of synoptic positivity is for the most part bound to be an unrealizable illusion. But the elimination of outright flaws and defects can conceivably afford a realistic prospect.

NOTE

1. *Metaphysics*, 1021b12–17.

Part IV

CONCLUSION

#38

Concluding Observations

Every distinctive domain of discourse is *semantically autonomous*: each is at liberty to lay down its own communicative ground rules. The fact that others proceed differently presents no obstacle here. However, the fact remains that one cannot transplant terms from one context of discussion to another without explaining their changed presuppositions and implications in that new conceptual environment. And in the case of philosophy this creates special problems when these explanations are more than minimally complex. For then we are really no longer dealing with the concept at issue, but have changed the subject to some other sort of thing. But just this is likely to be a very problematic enterprise, virtually foredoomed to failure by the consideration that philosophical usage must be precise, whereas the use of terms in everyday discourse is flexible and irregular.

For a philosophical concept that cannot ultimately be explained in otherwise available terminology is thereby ultimately unintelligible. And a philosophical doctrine whose use of terms violates their basic ground rules of understanding without due explanation—whose knowledge or truth or justice is something different from what is ordinarily meant—is thereby untenable. Philosophers can coherently assign *different values and priorities* to the things at issue with our ordinary terms but it cannot coherently cast the linguistic properties to the wind. A speculative philosopher can elevate dogs above lions in his scheme of things and classify dogs as "the king of beasts," but he cannot make lions into dogs. He can argue that the things ordinarily seen as virtues should be re-evaluated as vices, but he cannot make *vice into virtue*.

Philosophers traditionally aspire to provide *real definitions* of terms—definitions which are not arbitrary conventional stipulations but which capture (represent) the pre-established meaning of terms as reflected in their actual employment.

There is, in fact, a good deal that can go wrong when philosophers employ everyday vocabulary in their own elucidations. The possibilities here prominently include:

- *Terminological inflation*: using a term of limited applicability well outside its ordinary range.
- *Terminological contraction*: restricting the use of a term more narrowly than its standard use would warrant.
- *Terminological distortion*: employing terms in a way at variance with their established usage.

To be sure, all such departures are unproblematic if conscientiously explained and carefully accounted for. But when it is not done, and renders one attuned and indeed invalid to continue under the (mis-)impression that the discussion addresses the concepts at issue in the established terminology, then what is being committed is a kind of expository slight-of-hand that verges on verbal fraud. From the present perspective, such a mistaken allocation of meaning is akin to a mistaken allocation of funds.

Its linkage to the pre-systemic issues of our experiential world, which after all, set the stage for our philosophizing are an inherent aspect of what makes philosophy the enterprise it is. Of course, philosophers are free to invent their own language and to introduce their own technical terminology. But if they are to use it for communicating with the rest of us, they must explain it to us, and this is something they have to do in a language that we can understand or in the language of the familiar discourse of everyday life. A philosopher cannot at one and the same time practice his craft and forsake the everyday and scientific conceptions that provide the stage setting of his discipline. The philosopher is thus often caught between a rock and a hard place—unwilling merely to endorse those experientially biased conceptions of pre-philosophical usage and yet unable to dispense with because the core problems of the field take their root and draw their life from them.[1] And employing established terminology in a manner that involves unexplained departures from their established sense is a form of misrepresentation. The object of a concept audit is to reveal this sort of transgression where it exists.

Concept auditing admits of two special modes of application—among others. One of these is based on the stance of saying to a philosopher "If you are purporting to discuss an already-familiar sort of thing—knowledge, beauty, justice, right, or whatever—then you cannot sever the connection with the standardly established meaning of the pertinent terminology. For if your claims part ways with the realities of established usage, then you are at odds the matters you claim to address, and are in fact changing the subject." After all, insofar as a philosophical discussion purports to address the idea that is at issue in a familiar term, it cannot but respect the understandings that function so as to give that term its meaning.

And so, one particularly serious finding of an audit emerges when it reveals a defalcation by a philosopher in that his treatment of some concept is at odds with the ground rules that govern its established usage in ordinary discourse. This is in essence a fraud because in purporting to deal with a familiar idea the discussion actually deals with something else that is recognizably different from it.

NOTE

1. On these issues see the section on "Ideal Language Philosophy versus Ordinary Language Philosophy" in the introduction to Richard Rorty's anthology, *The Linguistic Turn* (Chicago: University of Chicago Press, 1967).

Bibliography

D. M. Armstrong, *A Combinational Theory of Possibility* (Cambridge: Cambridge University Press, 1989).

J. L. Austin, *How to Do Things with Words* (Harvard MA: Harvard University Press, 1962).

Jean-Christophe Bardout, *Penser l'existence* (Paris: J. Vrin, 2013).

Damian Caluori, *Plotinus on the Soul* (Cambridge: Cambridge University Press, 2015).

Roderick M. Chisholm, *Person and Object* (La Salle: Open Court, 1976).

R. M. Dancy, *Sense and Contradiction: A Study in Aristotle* (Dordrecht: D. Reidel, 1975).

D. C. Dennett, *Elbow Room: The Varieties of Free Will Worth Wanting* (Cambridge: MIT Press, 1984).

D. C. Dennett, *Freedom Evolves* (New York: Viking, 2003).

René Descartes, *Discourse on Method*, tr. by John Veitch (London: Everyman's Library, 1912).

Paul Diesing, *Science and Ideology in the Policy Sciences* (New York: Aldine, 1982).

Edmund Gettier, "Is Justified True Belief Knowledge," *Analysis*, vol. 23 (1963), pp. 121–123.

Thomas Hobbes, *The Elements of Law Natural and Political and Human Nature*, ed. by J. C. A. Gaskin (New York: Oxford University Press, 1994).

Immanuel Kant, Metaphysical Principles of Nature (Metaphysische Anfangsgründe der Tugendlehre).

Immanuel Kant, *Practical Philosophy*, tr. Mary T. McGregor (Cambridge: Cambridge University Press, 1996).

G. Kirk, J. E. Raven, and M. Schofield, *The Pre-Socratic Philosophers* (Cambridge: Cambridge University Press, 1957).

Michael Krausz (ed.), *Is There a Single Right Interpretation*, (University Park, PA: Pennsylvania State University Press, 2002).

Diogenes Laertius, *Lives of Eminent Philosopher*, (tr. R. D. Hicks) (Cambridge Mass: Harvard University Press (Loeb Classical Library, 1928).

Keith Lehrer, *Knowledge* (Oxford: Clarendon Press, 1974).

George Mavrodes, "On Deriving the Normative from the Non-Normative," *Papers of the Michigan Academy of Arts and Sciences*, vol. 53 (1968), pp. 353–365.

John Stuart Mill, *On Liberty and Utilitarianism* (New York: Knopf: Distributed by Random House, 1992).

Fred D. Miller, Jr., and Nicholas D. Smith, *Thought Probes* (Englewood Cliffs, Prentice Hall, 1980).

Plato, *Republic*.

Plato, *Theaetetus*.

Plotinus, *Enneads*.

Derek J. Price. *Little Science, Big Science* (New York: Columbia University Press, 1963).

Frank P. Ramsey, *The Foundations of Mathematics and Other Logical Essays*, ed. by R. B. Braithwaite (London: K. Paul, Trench, Trubner & co., 1931).

Nicholas Rescher, *Introduction to Value Theory* (Engelwood Cliffs: Prentice Hall, 1969).

Nicholas Rescher, Scientific Progress (Oxford: Blackwell, 1978).

Nicholas Rescher, *Philosophical Standardism* (Pittsburgh: University of Pittsburgh Press, 1994).

Nicholas Rescher, *Philosophy and Phenomenological Research*, vol. 71 (2005), pp. 392–398.

Richard Rorty, *The Linguistic Turn* (Chicago: University of Chicago Press, 1967).

Bertrand Russell, *The Problems of Philosophy* (London and New York: Oxford University Press, 1912).

Sydney Shoemaker and Richard Swinburne, *Personal Identity* (Oxford: Blackwell, 1984).

Spinoza, *Ethics*.

Francisco Suarez, *Metaphysical Disputations* (1597.)

J. O. Urmson, "On Grading," *Mind*, vol. 59, (1950), pp. 145–169.

J. O, Urmson, et al., "J. L. Austin" in R. Rorty (ed.), *The Linguistic Turn* (Chicago: University of Chicago Press, 1967).

G. J. Warnock, *J. L. Austin* (London; New York: Routledge, 1989).

Max Weber, *Der Sinn der Wertfreiheit* (Leibzig: *Logos* series, Vol. VII, 1917).

Ludwig Wittgenstein, *On Certainty* (Oxford: Basil Blackwell, 1961).

Ludwig Wittgenstein, *Tractatus Logico-philosophicus* (New York: Humanities Press, 1961).

George K. Zipf, *Human Behavior and the Principle of Least Effort* (Cambridge, Mass., Addison-Wesley Press, 1949).

Index

About the Author

Nicholas Rescher was born in Hagen, Germany, and moved to the USA in 1938 at the age of ten. He is Distinguished University Professor of Philosophy at the University of Pittsburgh where he has also served as Chairman of the Philosophy Department and a Director of the Center for Philosophy of Science. In a productive research career extending over six decades, he has established himself as a systematic philosopher with over one hundred books to this credit, ranging over all areas of philosophy, with sixteen of them translated from English into eight other languages. His work envisions a dialectical tension between our synoptic aspirations for useful knowledge and our human limitations as finite inquirers. The elaboration of this project represents a many-sided approach to fundamental philosophical issues that weaves together threads of thought from the philosophy of science, and from continental idealism and American pragmatism. And apart from this larger program Rescher has made various specific contributions to logic including the "Rescher quantifier" and the conception autodescriptive systems of many-valued logic, the history of logic (the medieval Arabic theory of modal syllogistic), to the theory of knowledge (epistemetrics as a quantitative approach in theoretical epistemology), and to the philosophy of science (the theory of a logarithmic retardation of scientific progress). Rescher has also worked in the area of futuristics, and along with Olaf Helmer and Norman Dalkey is co-inaugurator of the so-called Delphi method of forecasting. The *Encyclopedia of Bioethics* credits Rescher with writing one of the very first articles in the field. An expert on the philosophy of Leibniz he was responsible for the recovery and restruction of Leibniz's 1670s cipher machine. Fourteen books about Rescher's philosophy have been published in five languages, and ten doctoral dissertations have be dedicated to his work.

Rescher earned his doctorate at Princeton in 1951 while still at the age of twenty-two—a record for Princeton's Department of Philosophy. He has served as a President of the American Philosophical Association, of the American Catholic Philosophy Association, of the American G. W. Leibniz Society, of the C. S. Peirce Society, and of the American Metaphysical Society as well as Secretary General of the International Union of History and Philosophy of Sciences. He was the founding editor of the *American Philosophical Quarterly*. An honorary member of Corpus Christi College, Oxford, he has been elected to membership in the American Academy of Arts and Sciences, the Royal Asiatic Society of Great Britain, the European Academy of Arts and Sciences (Academia Europaea), the Royal Society of Canada, the Institut International de Philosophie, and several other learned academies. Having held visiting lectureships at Oxford, Constance, Salamanca, Munich, and Marburg, he has been awarded fellowships by the Ford, Guggenheim, and National Science Foundations. He is the recipient of eight honorary degrees from universities on three continents. He was awarded the Alexander von Humboldt Prize for Humanistic Scholarship in 1984, the Belgian Prix Mercier in 2005, and the Aquinas Medal of the American Catholic Philosophical Association in 2007, the Founder's Medal of the Metaphysical Society of America in 2016, and the Helmholtz Medal of the Germany Academy of Sciences (Berlin/Brandenburg) in 2016. In 2011, he received the premier cross of the Order of Merit (Bundesverdienstkreuz Erster Klasse) of the Federal Republic of Germany in recognition of contributions to philosophy and to German-American cooperation in this domain.